BEYOND THE CASTLE DOORS

A SOUL QUEST FOR THE HOLY GRAIL

BEYOND THE CASTLE DOORS

A SOUL QUEST FOR THE HOLY GRAIL

by

Maria Morris O'Brien, M.Ed, &
Debi King McMartin, M.A.

*with Theological Reflection and Afterword
by Carolyn Sur, SSND, PhD*

FINDHORN PRESS

First published by Findhorn Press in 2007

ISBN 978-1-84409-110-2

Edited by Magaer Lennox
Cover and interior design by Damian Keenan
Printed and bound in the USA

1 2 3 4 5 6 7 8 9 10 11 12 13 12 11 10 09 08 07

Published by
Findhorn Press
305a The Park, Findhorn
Forres IV36 3TE
Scotland, UK

Telephone
+44-1309-690582
Fax
+44-1309-690036

info@findhornpress.com
www.findhornpress.com

DISCLAIMER

This story is a work of allegorical fiction using fictitious characters as models for the reader. The specific characters portrayed in this work are strictly the authors' creations and any resemblance to true-life persons is purely coincidental.

DEDICATION

To our beloved Sophia
and our beloved children

"When he established the heavens I was there,
when he marked out the vault over the face of the deep;
When he made firm the skies above,
when he fixed fast the foundations of the earth;
When he set for the sea its limit,
so that the waters should not transgress his command;
Then was I beside him as his craftsman,
and I was his delight day by day,
Playing before him all the while,
playing on the surface of his earth;
and I found delight in the sons of men."

— Proverbs 8:27-3 [1]

"In my Father's house there are many dwelling places.
If there were not, would I have told you that I am
going to prepare a place for you?
And if I go and prepare a place for you,
I will come back again and take you to myself,
so that where I am you also may be.
Where (I) am going you know the way."

— John 14:2-4 [2]

CONTENTS

PART I

PART II

SECTION 1
Sophia References

CONTENTS

CONTENTS

PREFACE AND ACKNOWLEDGMENTS

We began writing this book in 1999. Both of us had other careers at the time and many other worldly responsibilities. Though we had little time to devote to this project, we both felt the need to continue writing as our families filled their time without us. By the grace of God and in God's time we were able to finish this work in the winter of 2005. We prayerfully worked nearly every Sunday afternoon for six years as it evolved. In our brainstorming sessions, we agreed to present this information through story. We hoped for a user-friendly guidebook for spiritual growth and development, and one that would serve our readers in their understanding of some profound concepts. If this book affects one life for the good, then our time spent will be well served.

We would like to acknowledge all those who have assisted us in this work and thank them for their insights and wisdom. Over the course of six years, the following individuals spent time educating us, reading our many drafts, and believing in us and what we hoped to accomplish: Father Murray Clayton, Margaret Glenn, Jim McGill, Sister Carolyn Sur, Glenn Ann Carmody, Ann Nunley, Bill Hale, Kaye Lindauer, Candy Peavy, Bill O'Brien, Dottie King, Lyn Morgan, Jim Davis, Jerry Wright, and Cissy Cunningham. We especially want to thank our families for their love and support as we worked together to bring you *Beyond the Castle Doors: A Soul Quest for the Holy Grail*.

We acknowledge and thank our beloved 16th century mystic, St. Teresa of Avilla, for her book *The Interior Castle*. We believe our book was divinely inspired and her book served as a template for us in our writing. This is just one more example of how the underground stream of consciousness serves us all.

***

Introduction

BEYOND THE CASTLE DOORS serves as a guide through the labyrinth of growth and transformation. So many people resist entering "the castle," an inner world of myth and archetypes, a place of confrontation with the shadows and light of the unconscious. Fear is usually the cause of resistance, and a lack of awareness that staying stuck will affect their bodies, mind, and spirit like the slow erosion of water against stone. The cost to their emotional, psychological, and spiritual health can be enormous.

A question that lies before us is: How do we continue to grow in faith, let go and heal from the wounds of the past, remain optimistic about the future, and live this wondrous gift called *life*? How do we set our hearts and minds on our eternal life instead of what appears before us each day?

How many people begin their adult lives with glittering expectations for the future: expectations of a perfect marriage to the ideal partner, a fulfilling job, and children who will never give them a moment's worry? Oh, they know of others who do not fare so well, but somehow they feel different, special. They were destined to escape the pain, tragedy, and craziness of others who are less than blessed. Somehow they've avoided the madness by marrying smart, choosing a lucrative profession, and swimming in the better gene pool.

We grew up believing in the ideal, the dream that had been instilled in us by family, teachers, and institutions, and reinforced by movies, theater, magazines, and books. If they all say it, then it must be so. Our authority remained outside of ourselves – that is where we were taught to find power. Far be it for us to question those who know.

As females, we've been taught to look attractive and talk sweetly so everyone will like us – especially the one we choose to be our very own prince. Remember when we all breathed a sigh of relief as the glass slipper slid onto Cinderella's slender foot with such ease? That's exactly the expectation we carried with us to the moment our wedding band slipped on so smoothly – everything would be perfect from this moment forward. But have you ever stopped to think about what happened to Cinderella after the lavish wedding when she stepped *beyond the castle doors*? That is where the fairy tale ends and reality begins.

If she's like most of us, Cinderella woke up one day to discover she had traded one form of imprisonment for another. How many of us have lived for the dream, only to awaken and discover that our dream has been shattered? We felt disoriented, lost, and in tremendous pain. We don't know what happened to our beautiful dream and don't have a clue about how to begin picking up the pieces of our lives, much less how to put them back together.

Many don't want to let go of the tenuous illusion on which they've based their lives. So they hang onto the dream and keep trying to get it right, only to have it shattered again and again.

Has anyone married the handsome prince and lived happily ever after? Most often life has become a tedious round of working frenziedly for worldly comforts, constantly shopping for possessions, living in the expected image of success, and perhaps trying to temper the escalating feud with the dysfunctional family. It seems like life hands over one brutal reality at a time to test one's abilities to endure, trust, and continue. Most of these "striving for happily-ever-after" stories lead to the conclusion that there is no magic elixir for happily ever after. Because reality has not met our expectation, we end up tired, in despair, depressed beyond measure.

When the glass slipper splinters into a thousand slivers, we grab our glass of wine, shop for distraction, change spouses, inhale cigarettes, or consume our drug of choice to numb out the world for awhile. Frequently we use some form of addiction or distraction to avoid the inevitable pain that comes with change and subsequent growth. But the pain of growth is part of the mystery, part of the grief process of changing a pattern that has been a part of us for too long.

As with most young women living *beyond* the castle doors, it wasn't long before each day of living in this honest reality became an arduous task. What happened after my honeymoon was over – when I could no longer claim ignorance or live the unconscious bliss state?

My journey through healing into wholeness began at age thirty-one, directly following the birth of my third child, my only son. Looking back, I realize that painful personal relationships, family dysfunction, and blatant dishonesty amongst family members threw me into such a painful state that it manifested in physical disease. I knew that the old dream was not working. Somehow I had to create a healthier dream, a new mind-set on which to base my life.

Introduction

Unbeknownst to me at the time, my bodily symptoms were a physical manifestation of the deep psychological and spiritual pain I was experiencing in the outer world but repressing in the inner. I've learned that it is easier for the ego to use the distraction of physical pain to keep you from looking at a pain that's much greater – the truth of the pain within. Honestly embracing the truth, though painful, will eventually set you free.

As a young married woman I was jolted from the nurturing arms of my family of origin, a haven of love and support, to the rude awakening that some relationships, family systems, and friendships can be driven by greed, jealousy, and dishonesty that result in betrayal, rejection, and abandonment. I was emotionally unequipped to deal with the reality that these relationships are not always harbingers of love and support and are not necessarily kind to one another. The pain I felt as a result of that betrayal rocked my world. I watched Biblical stories like Joseph with his dream coat and Cain and Abel play out before my very eyes. Mythological stories like those of Medusa and Medea were reenacted in a contemporary version and I realized that negative life forces often wear the mask of a loved one – one whose *modus operandi* is to kiss, then betray.

When my physical body was too pained, depressed, and fatigued to go on, I collapsed with exhaustion and surrendered to a painful journey of self-discovery and healing. Now I know that strong moral character is built through crisis and that at some point in everyone's life, they will be knocked flat on their back, or at least to their knees. How a person responds to the crisis will determine whether the crisis develops the character, or the character becomes the crisis. If one does not psychologically and spiritually pick up the cross and walk to seek the good, the crisis will become his identity – the victim identity. In victim identity, the character becomes the crisis, thus an endless cycle of despair or addiction, generating a very long "dark night of the soul."

I have learned to understand and appreciate the blessings generated from the work in crisis and the opportunity it brings to deepen my relationship with God. I also came to realize that some of the most difficult relationships and experiences became my greatest teachers. In my heart I agreed to present this fictional story in a manner that serves the readers – with the intention for everything good.

On one blessed day, I read the passage from *Ephesians 6:10-20* [3] describing the full armor of God. The following words jumped off the page, into my heart:

"Finally, draw your strength from the Lord and from his mighty power. Put on the armor of God so that you may be able to stand firm against the tactics of the devil. For our struggle is not with flesh and blood but with the principalities, with the powers, with the world rulers of this present darkness, with the evil spirits in the heavens. Therefore, put on the armor of God, that you may be able to resist on the evil day and, having done everything, to hold your ground. So stand fast with your loins girded in truth, clothed with righteousness as a breastplate, and your feet shod in readiness for the gospel of peace. In all circumstances, hold faith as a shield, to quench all (the) flaming arrows of the evil one.

And take the helmet of salvation and the sword of the Spirit, which is the word of God. With all prayer and supplication, pray at every opportunity in the Spirit. To that end, be watchful with all perseverance and supplication for all the holy ones and also for me, that speech may be given me to open my mouth, to make known with boldness the mystery of the gospel for which I am an ambassador in chains, so that I may have the courage to speak as I must."

By opening my mind and heart to the spirit of goodness, many serendipitous events and experiences brought to light the journey of so many wise women. I was introduced to the mystery of the Black Madonna, the wisdom of Sophia, and the many icons of feminine spiritual energy that I so desperately needed to mentor and guide me in this process. I realized I was not alone, and just as importantly, this is not only my journey but the journey of every woman.

In the story that follows, you will meet Eva. One night when she thinks she cannot live through another day, she has a dream that changes her life. A silent knight in shining armor beckons her to enter through a heavy wooden door and into the chambers of a large medieval castle. Here she meets her Knight. He serves as guide and protector, allowing her to feel safe during the frightening journey into her own dark shadow. The dream Knight dresses Eva in the full armor of God, the same *armor* that protects us from harm every day. Soon she meets another guide, the wise and nurturing Sophia – mother, daughter, and holy soul of her being.

Introduction

Sigmund Freud and Carl Jung helped us to understand the importance and significance of our dream world for psychological and spiritual growth. Carl Jung helped us to realize the significance of the dreams in both our personal and collective unconscious. Through dream language and its meaningful symbolism, we are able to understand the world of the unconscious. It is here, in the quiet depths of our soul that we are able to understand God's voice and feel the much-needed protection in order to continue the journey into our own essence, the journey to our soul.

One contemplative yet active nun, St. Teresa of Avila, served to mentor my personal journey *beyond the castle doors*. Her book, *The Interior Castle*, served as a labyrinth through my own inner world. Just as Eva finds her way in the story, I opened the gates to the "interior castle" and walked through the seven chambers. I discovered the sacred path that many women have journeyed before me. Women from every culture, from every point in history unconsciously have lived this story to individuation, even before the time of Christ. Without a conscious realization, my own ancestors, the ancient Greeks, told stories that lived on into the future and became age-old mythological truths. This was their way of experiencing God – through the goddess stories. This work will repeat ancient stories in modern genre.

Eva's castle journey will help answer these questions for the woman today in a profound, experiential way. Eva's story and her dream that follows are written in primitive form – much like our ancient myths, fantasies, or fairy tales. This voyage through the labyrinth serves as a guide and template for others poised on the brink of change. A trail of thread will be left behind, and landmarks established along the way to make the journey easier. It is the re-creation of the myth long forgotten, long repressed, and whose re-emergence is much needed. Through Eva's experience, she developed a new loving pattern in her psyche and soul – a pattern, which changed the way she viewed the world, ultimately allowing her life energy to flow purely. Every woman has her own Cinderella story. The story that follows relates Eva's unique experiences and what happens to her *beyond the castle doors*.

My wish for you during your journey, my friend, is to find hope in the lessons that come. May you find your life mission, fulfillment, peace, and ultimately contentment in your own interior castle. It is with great reverence and love for the spirit of goodness and all of creation that we respectfully present to you: *Beyond the Castle Doors: A Soul Quest for the Holy Grail.*

PART I

Eva's Story

"Does not Wisdom call, and Understanding raise her voice?
On the top of the heights along the road, at the crossroads
she takes her stand;
By the gates at the approaches of the city, in the entryways
she cries aloud:
'To you, O men, I call; my appeal is to the children of men.
You simple ones, gain resource, you fools, gain sense.
'Give heed! for noble things I speak; honesty opens my lips."

— Proverbs 8:1-6[4]

EVA, RAISED IN A TRADITIONAL working-class Pennsylvania family, had yearned for adventure her whole life. She couldn't wait to go off to college, to see the world, to *change* the world. The last thing she was looking for was love.

And then it happened – the moment she laid eyes on Chris, she knew her life had changed forever. Eva felt struck by a bolt of lightning – everything inside of her shifted. He was, without a doubt, the most handsome, charismatic man she'd ever encountered. His piercing blue eyes penetrated straight to her soul the instant they were formally introduced. Eva stopped breathing. She couldn't speak. Call it love at first sight or intuitive knowing, but in that instant, she knew she would marry this man. Eva had met her destiny. Replaying the scenario in her mind after so many years still makes her smile, and her heart rate soar! Now she re-remembers her story, a glimpse back in time at significant crossroads, some filled with pain, many filled with joy...

Playing out her fate is fun and exciting for Eva. Several weeks pass before Chris calls (finally!) to ask Eva for a date, enough time for her to play all kinds of adventurous scenarios out in her imagination. She spends every waking moment planning what to wear, what to say, and how to act. Not having any impressive clothes to wear, Eva frantically scours friends' closets before finding the perfect outfit – a red, slinky dress that makes her feel sexy and dazzling.

Chris picks her up in his shiny red sports car (which conveniently matches the slinky red dress!) and heads straight to the local take-out drive-through liquor store. Though Eva's not a drinker, she smiles sweetly and says, "I'll have what you're having."

They talk about their lives – and what a contrast. Chris is part of a wealthy, aristocratic family living a lavish lifestyle replete with mansion, servants, and a fleet of vehicles at their disposal. Eva was raised in a small industrial town by parents who are common laborers. Though there was always an abundance of food on the table and lots of love, there was not much of anything else. They washed their own clothes, drove early model cars, made their own beds, cleaned the toilets, and cooked the vegetables grown in a small garden plot in the backyard. For the life of her, Eva cannot understand what Chris finds appealing about plain ole her.

Chris and Eva live the fairy tale replete with falling in love and all the ingredients for the recipe of "happily ever after." They have a royal wedding of sorts, their families presenting an interesting contrast in cultures, then settle in Chris' hometown. Eva has no reason to doubt that she's found her prince, will enter the castle, *her* castle, and live happily ever after.

Then the castle doors slam shut behind her – and she begins the work of learning the hard, bittersweet, beautiful lessons of life – *beyond the castle doors...*

A decade had seemed to pass very quickly while settling into marriage and family. On this cloudy winter day, Eva heads to a neighborhood church. When she has heavy-duty praying to do, she attends church in the faith tradition in which she was born and raised. On this day she is on her hands and knees, inhaling the sweet aroma of incense, listening intently to the mesmeric cantors chanting ancient scripture, and watching the candles flicker in the sand trays.

A strong sense of God's presence permeates the atmosphere and wraps a comforting cloak of peace around her. She's embraced on all sides by family, anchoring Eva in their loving support. Her heart is at peace. The words of the elderly priest echo in her mind, "When your will is in his will, you will find peace." Truer words were never spoken. As she scans the bowed heads of her children, she is grateful for their presence. Then she recalls a vivid scene, the source of the most painful time of her life.

Eva's Story

In another person's home, Eva is surrounded by the finest appointments the world has to offer. An argument ensues, the heated conflict escalating toward an explosive confrontation between Chris and another. Chris is being accused of serving as ringleader in opposition to family dictates – dictates he believes to be destructive. Destructive enough to destroy the family business, the business Chris had been tending since his father's death. Eva notices her own heart palpitations, a physical manifestation of her inner anxiety as she listens to the escalating feud.

With heartfelt emotion, fielding the brunt of the pain motivating both parties, Eva pleads with the family members to work toward a resolution that will benefit everyone, beginning with loving each other unconditionally; and resist using the withdrawal of love as a form of punishment for not getting their own way. Her efforts are fruitless. Her heart grows heavy with the awareness that the consequences of the lack of resolution could be a painful family separation – one that could grow wider with time. She feels the pain of the innocent victims who will feel the void in the fabric of family – the fabric that holds our society and world together with fragile threads. Eva understands too well that when the threads are broken, it leaves a hole that is felt for generations to come.

The room swells with the sounds of virulent words, the wrath and vengeance palpable in the air. Eva suddenly feels nauseous from the dark, consuming power. The puzzle pieces fall in place and Eva sees the blinding truth. Her eyes are open and she understands. She feels alone, and very frightened.

Eva cooks something nutritious for Sunday lunch, a family tradition and celebration of family time together. She treasures fond memories of her mother making home-cooked meals every day when Eva lived at home. Her mother's voice still whispers softly in Eva's heart, gently nudging her to keep up the tradition. Her mother never used a recipe, but everything that came out of her kitchen tasted delicious. Eva felt fortunate to have had a loving mother who modeled Christ's love by her devotion to family. But having a loving mother was only part of Eva's understanding of the meaning of unconditional love.

Now that Eva is a mother, she cannot understand the contrast between the love in her own heart, the love her mother generates, and the malice projected by dysfunctional patterns she sees in other individuals or unhealthy systems. She wonders what happens to the hearts and minds of human beings to create this pain and chaos, inflicting it onto their own flesh and blood. Eva ponders her own sinfulness and quietly prays: "Lord, Jesus Christ, have mercy on me. I am a sinner. Open my eyes to you and show me the way of the light, the way of wisdom."

Eva thinks that evil results when negative energy is allowed to build on its own momentum and takes on a life force of its own – much like the energy a tornado builds as it becomes a unit of force – carving a path of destruction through everything in its wake. The same dynamic can play out in an individual, marriage, community or country – until the strength of the positive intervenes and becomes strong enough to break the pattern of systemic evil, thereby breaking the bondage of "the sins of the father." Now she understands the meaning of the Lord's Prayer passage "...and deliver us from evil."

Is this systemic evil part of what we have to experience on this earth to understand and appreciate deeply abiding and genuine love? Maybe so, because without these deeply wounding and disappointing experiences, Eva knows that she could never have come to know the Creator in the profound way he exists in her life today. Our Lord would, no doubt, have remained a remote and omnipotent force, personally unapproachable, had Eva not been knocked flat on her back. Without the excruciating pain, she would not have needed him to fill that place, nor experienced the sublime nature of infinite, unconditional, perfect love.

Only after going through this experience, excruciatingly painful as it was, is Eva able to fully understand the universal yearning in everyone to find God within, as she became aware of her own yearning to find the heaven within. Out of this awareness, she moved forward to meet the call to know and walk with God in every moment, every aspect of her life.

Eva's Dream

EVA FELT PARALYZED on the sterile, impersonal steel hospital bed. The doctors could find nothing wrong. So why was it so painful to blink or even touch her hair?

With the silent question an intuitive flash suddenly came to her. Her disease, her ailment, was a disease of the soul – a disease that medical tests had no devices to measure or diagnose. But it was as insidious and deadly as any plague. Her spirit was dying. And she had to find a way to get it back. She knew she had to remove herself from the dark force of painful dysfunctional relationships and personal conflict, this Medusa-like energy that threatened to consume her and her family. But how? Then she remembered God's voice, his promise. Call him and he would come. She needed him again now. This time she would go into prayer, even if it meant excruciating pain.

Eva carefully slid her shaking legs over the side of the bed and crumpled to the floor. She lifted herself onto her knees and brought her hands together. "Dear God," Eva began, "I do trust in you completely. Please, oh, please guide me to the next step."

Eva began her deep breathing. After about eight breaths her brain felt giddy. She must have been oxygen deprived for a long time. The room darkened suddenly and she saw a huge ball of light roll toward her, stopping at her feet. Like a fireworks sparkler, the light sputtered and dissipated, crackling as it dissolved. Eva blinked, her vision adjusting to the darkness. A medieval knight stood before her, shining in full armor. She could not see his face for the helmet, but his voice echoed strong and kind, deep and resonant.

"Eva, I'm here to help and protect you. Trust me." the Knight's comforting voice whispered to her again. "I'm going to take you to a place of healing, where no harm can be done to you. You will have an opportunity to grow, develop, strengthen, heal, and understand your mission here on earth in a very short period of what you call time. All I ask is that you follow me with faith and trust.

I will be suiting you with full armor and weapons in due time – spiritual armor for the journey ahead. You will be protected by the white light that I place around you, a powerful force that will protect you from predators and negative forces. I am going now. I will come for you in your dream tonight."

The Knight faded slowly and the lights flickered on. Eva blinked and wondered if she had been dreaming. No, the Knight was real, as real as anything in the room. She suddenly felt the first glimmer of hope that she had felt in a long, long time and an incredible feeling of peace descended upon her. She knew she must sleep. Sleep would restore her, and lead her into the dream that would be the first step in her healing.

The nurse opened the door, "Are you okay, Eva?"

"Yes, why?" she answered.

"The hospital just had a two-minute blackout. Our generators kept the equipment active but we're checking on all the patients to make sure everyone's all right."

"Thanks." said Eva, tucking herself deep into the hospital blankets. She then fell into the deepest slumber she had ever known.

In her dream, Eva awoke to the fecund scent of the earth and the cheerful cacophony of a chorus of birds. Still a bit dazed, she sat up and looked around the enormous emerald forest. A burst of floral color met her gaze as she watched a dirt path lined with an abundance of wild flowers unfurl before her eyes. She looked down at her clothes and felt the strange material. Clothed in an unfamiliar brown muslin skirt with an embroidered vest and soft leather shoes to match, Eva fingered the leather canteen hung from a thin robe belt around her waist. *The Knight. The promise. Trust him.*

Eva slowly made her way down the path. So enthralled was she with the surrounding beauty that it suddenly dawned on her that she felt no pain, only wonder and excitement! She felt like Alice in Wonderland after falling through the rabbit hole to another world! She trod lightly on the path leading her out of the forest and into dazzling sunlight. A beautiful castle of sparkling gold stone shone before her. A moat full of water surrounded it. A tiny wood-and-rope swinging bridge invited her to cross. "*Trust me.*" *the Knight's comforting voice whispered to her again.*

Eva stepped forward tentatively. The rope bridge looked old and rickety but she moved forward on faith, embracing uncertainty. He had promised her safety. She walked up the twenty-one steps to the enormous wooden door of the castle. It was slightly ajar, as if someone was expecting her. Then she saw the shadow of the Knight behind the door. He said nothing, only waited for her but somehow she felt very safe. She knew she must ask a question for entry.

"What must I do to be healed?" she asked.

The Knight opened the door and motioned for her to come in. In silence he led her to the magnificent banquet room. On the long wooden table was a virtual feast of culinary riches – whole-roasted chicken, lamb, pork on a skewer, an array of vegetables, and fruits of every color and family.

The Knight spoke to her through his silence. "*Eva, soon you will be well enough to partake of all the delicacies you see on this table and all the fruits the world has to offer. But first you must do your work.*"

As beautiful and delightful as the food appeared on the table, Eva had no appetite.

As if reading her thoughts, the Knight said, again through his silence, "*Soon you will have an appetite, Eva, for the right food at the right time. When you do your inner work, you will automatically desire the food that reflects the fruit of your spirit, the fruit you will work very hard to attain. At this time you would be unable to digest it, for your body is not in a state of readiness for it. It is time for us to make our way into the first chamber of the castle, the first phase of your healing – the red chamber.*"

The First Chamber

Red chamber – sacral energy center

"Later generations have seen the light, have dwelt in the
land, But the way to understanding they have not known,
they have not perceived her paths, or reached her;
their offspring were far from the way to her.
She has not been heard of in Canaan, nor seen in Teman.
    The sons of Hagar who seek knowledge on earth,
the merchants of Midian and Teman, the phrasemakers
seeking knowledge, These have not known the way to
wisdom, nor have they her paths in mind."

— Baruch 3:20-23 [5]

THE KNIGHT held the stone door slightly ajar as he led Eva down the massive
corridor to the first chamber. Ruby stones formed the walls on both sides of the
hall. The Knight's armor clinked and echoed loudly through the corridor. Soon
they reached a massive room on the dungeon floor, underground. Descending
a slanted floor, she knew instinctively that it was time for her next question,
which would allow her entry into the red chamber.

"What is my task?" Eva asked aloud, the words tumbling from her lips without even having to think about the question.

The Knight finally spoke aloud. "Your task is to breathe and observe. This is
the red chamber of your birth, the sacral energy at the bottom of your spine,
the root of your existence on earth, your ancestry, and the collective inherited
gifts from all of time. In your mother's womb you were surrounded by water
and baptized into life in this world. The red is the blood, the life force, and also
the fire that courses through your veins, the blood of your mother that still
flows within you. It is the water of the Sophia energy – that of the great mother who also nourishes you. You have already been baptized with the water. Now

you are being baptized with the fire. Fire burns, fire causes pain, but it also cauterizes negativity and evil. Do not be afraid to walk through the fire of the red chamber as it will cleanse and purify you."

Eva asked, "What shall I call you?"

The Knight answered, "You may call me Father, as in priest. I am here and will always be here to protect you. However, it's also important that you know Sophia. She, the feminine, is to be as equally revered as the masculine. Upon meeting her, you will experience the counterpart of her within yourself, the divine feminine within. She will guide you with wisdom."

"How do I know what part of me is Sophia energy and how do I honor it?"

"This part of you will feel very natural," said the Knight in his soothing, mesmerizing voice. "Sophia energy is the nurturing, loving, creative, intuitive, flowing, soft, vulnerable, and receptive part of you – as it is part of everyone. When you honor, acknowledge, revere and nurture it, you become a whole and balanced human being, enhancing your own life and making the world a better place. The masculine part of your energy, the 'green man,' as it has been called, is the rational, the doer, the warrior, the protector, and serves as the container for the Sophia energy, the life force, the current. I represent the green man energy in total balance with the Sophia energy. You will meet Sophia soon. With every room you visit, I will bestow upon you a gift of armor to assist and protect. For the red room it will be your *shoes*."

The Knight handed her a pair of leather lace-up shoes that reminded her of moccasins. "This is your spiritual armor for the red chamber, to shod you for readiness of the spirit."

He held the door open and she entered a dark, windowless chamber bathed in glowing reddish light. The far wall sparkled with rubies.

The Knight spoke, "This is the first of the seven lessons of your spiritual journey. It is necessary that you become grounded in this chamber before you move on to the next ones. The red chamber is the foundation for everything you must do to live in a healthy, constructive manner while on this earth. This will not be your first and it will not be your last visit to this place. Your energy will always cycle back through this first chamber, even after it has been alchemically changed through the higher chambers of the castle. Your feet are fitted with readiness to receive truth for spiritual living and will help prevent you from falling into the deadly trap within this chamber, which could severely injure you and hinder your advancement."

Alarmed, Eva asked, "And what is this trap I must avoid?"

The First Chamber

Kindly, the Knight revealed, "The deadly sin is that of sloth. Trapped in sloth are those souls who resist moving forward, which is the natural way of the universe. This stagnation of energy prevents the flow from chamber to chamber in the castle. These souls get pulled into all the enticements of the first chamber. These things may become all-consuming attachments and addictions, and become destructive if they are being used to serve only man and his basic self-interested needs (*ego*), rather than the Creator (the great spirit). Sloth is not only a physical laziness but an inability to attend to the difficult problems that life presents. This sin is not easily recognized and when it is, individuals will find many different kinds of defense mechanisms or use mental distortions to serve their ego's wants and needs."

The Knight continued, "Your journey is everyone's journey. When your energy shifts and re-patterns and you encounter others and exchange energy with them, it will affect a positive change in them without your ever having to *do* anything. To experience directly, or become actualized, 'to be in the world but not of it', you can command to be *in* your body in the green haze. You need only to clasp your hands together, close your eyes, and repeat the word 'Become.' In this way, you can observe the experience without it affecting you and learn the lessons without the pain."

The Knight continued, "Observe the actions in the green haze for awhile in silence, then tell me what you see."

Eva looked around the chamber, fascinated. In every corner there were beautiful sofas, ornately carved furniture, stained-glass lamps, artifacts of all ages, all very pleasing to the senses. In the right corner, men played cards and slapped money on a table – placing bets, drinking ale, and laughing riotously all the while. In the far-left corner was a man fondling a tall, raven-haired woman with a heavily made-up face, and wearing a tight, short, shiny dress.

"Paris!" Eva exclaimed, waving to her.

The Knight chuckled. "She can't see you outside of the haze, Eva. Go ahead and 'Become'."

Eva closed her eyes as instructed, clasped her hands together, and said, "Become."

Suddenly she was in the haze, inside her body, but with different clothes. Paris spotted her quickly and ran through the haze to give her a hug. "Eva, what are you doing here?"

"Well...I think this is really a … dream …"

"Oh, never mind. Come on over here and meet Charlie and Pete." said Paris, leading Eva by the hand and pulling her over to a booth where two good-looking men waited.

Paris immediately slid into the seat next to Pete, sidling up to him flirtatiously. "Eva, meet Pete. He's my main man for the night."

Eva felt stunned. Paris had been her loyal friend for a long time, always fun and full of life. Whenever Eva had become too intense and serious about life, Paris had always pulled her out of it with her earthy, wild-woman ways. But Eva had never known her to be *this* wild – blatantly cavorting with someone other than her husband. Granted, Paris's husband, Phil, was less than personable and actually fairly cold, but he was a good man and took care of Paris. What has gotten into my friend? Eva wondered, worry creasing her brow.

"Eva," Paris leaned over and whispered in her ear, her breath reeking of bourbon, "lighten up, will you, girlfriend?"

Eva attempted a half-smile. Charlie smiled and moved closer to her. Eva inched toward the edge of her seat.

Charlie moved his head within inches of her face. "I've been asking Paris if she had a friend that she could set me up with. Then, *voila*, you appear out of thin air. If you don't mind me saying, you are the most gorgeous woman I have ever laid eyes on."

Eva looked down and fidgeted, suddenly feeling very uncomfortable. "Well, thank you, but I'm married. I have a house, three children, two dogs, uh; one is an Alaskan husky. He really has a hard time living in such a hot climate. We had to take him to the vet last week because he got this skin condition...."

Charlie took a drink and threw his head back, laughing. "Eva, I don't care if you're married. Hell, we're all married and nobody likes it. We're all stuck; so let's make the best of it. Life is short and we're all gonna die so why not have a little fun before we go? What do you say, girl?"

"I think it's time for me to go." Eva said, stumbling out of the booth. She ran toward the door. Paris came after her and grabbed her arm.

"Where in the hell do you think you're going, Miss Holy-er-than-thou?" Paris hissed.

"Paris, this is not me."

"What is 'you,' Eva? You're putting up with those family monsters that make your life a living hell. You deserve this – and you know it. What you need is a good, hot affair – with a real man like Charlie. You need to let your hair down, Eva, that's what's wrong with you."

Eva shut her eyes and clasped her hands together, wanting nothing more than to be out of here, away from this person she thought she knew. "Become." she said.

Eva opened her eyes, standing again beside the Knight, feeling relief. She looked through the haze to watch Paris slow dancing with Pete, her arms wrapped around him, their bodies grinding against each other in a feral-like heat.

Eva glanced around the rest of the chamber. In the middle sat a man counting and recounting his money and making notes on a pad of paper. It appeared that some people had already mastered this chamber. Toward the front of the room, far away from Paris and the bar, a family discussed their country's competitor having just won a gold medal at the Olympics. Pride filled their faces as they congratulated other winners from different countries seated at tables around them. Others were outfitted in garments and robes for the worship service in their church that evening. They seemed to rejoice in their sense of belonging.

"I can see it now, and I felt it when I was in the haze with Paris. The people up front look like they are thriving. The ones in the back look desperate, like Paris."

"Exactly!" said the Knight. "Those in the back are stuck. They are slothful in the fact that the lessons are up before them, but they have refused to learn. They have not accepted the challenge to tap into their own spiritual natures and allow the lifeblood of Sophia to animate them. They have accepted only the structure of this world, the masculine energy, as real. They believe only in what their five senses report to them. They have not opened the door leading from the first chamber to the rest of the castle. So they stay in this worldly chamber where their lives are limited."

"What about their emotional life?" asked Eva.

"Since their emotional security is dependent on life in this world and their spiritual nature has not been developed, most of them operate from the emotion of fear. It is difficult to find fulfillment in this life when fear is the engine that drives the machine. Many feel chronic anxiety because of constant worry, fear of loss – loss of income, loss of a family member, their own life, things, freedom, and loss of anything.

"The predominant energy pattern in this chamber is that of the Innocent. The Innocent accepts authority at face value, like a child does. The society in which you live is authority-driven. In some ways this is good, as it establishes law and order and provides rules to this game of life. However, external authority can become so dominating that it inhibits growth of the soul. This is where we find conflict between what is legal (rules of the game) versus what is moral or ethical. It is imperative that you learn to question everything, to formulate thoughts, opinions, and actions that resonate with your spirit. This requires moving away from full reliance on the rational mind to make all judgments and decisions, and learn to listen to the intuitive, the voice of the soul and the seat of the Sophia energy."

Captivated, yet puzzled, Eva asked, "How does that happen since we as individuals make up society? We *are* society."

"You are right, Eva. But our society also develops a soul and persona of its own, based on the collective souls and energy of the individuals constituting its very being. Despite astronomical advances in technology over the past twenty years, your society is in a very dis-eased state of psychological health. The collective focus has become that of production, which feeds individual greed and manifests in corporate greed on an enormous scale. Corporations have become the Goliaths of your society. In another chamber you will learn more about greed. However, it's important to mention it here for one reason. The deadly sin of sloth keeps one stuck in these and other negative patterns.

"Greed is nothing but a force of energy with a charge that creates suction, much like a vacuum, scooping out something else to attempt to fill a void within – a spiritual void. Greed is an impetuous and insatiable craving. Greed devours. The subtle and not-so-subtle implications are a mind-set that is static and refuses to change and transform – a mind-set that is stuck in the societal red chamber of the castle."

Eva was awestruck and excited about the opportunity to learn so much in a direct way. "What about going back to my life – my real life?"

The Knight chuckled, a glint of humor escaping from the chinks in his armor. "The only difference between our worlds, the dream world and your physical world, is in the rate of vibration of the energy levels."

"So our physical body is actually connected to other realms of existence?"

"Yes, things are not limited to what is apparent to our five physical senses. The universe is bathed and permeated by the Holy Spirit, divine energy, sometimes called *chi* or *prana*. This is the force that drives everything. The concept is really very simple but elusive to many.

"When your great scientist, Einstein, uncovered the theory of relativity – represented by the mathematical formula, $E=MC^2$, ie, Energy = Mass × Speed of Light^2 – humankind had no idea of the full-scale ramifications of this discovery. Much was developed from that formula, many positive forces in the world, but also weapons for mass destruction. So the knowledge has been a double-edged sword for humanity ever since. Collectively, the level of consciousness of the human race has not been raised to a vibratory level high enough to manage the formula properly. The hope now is for individuals like you to do your inner work, grow in your understanding, transform your life, and then help others to do this work as well. By understanding this energy phenomenon, universal consciousness is elevated. This is the last hope to save the human race from mass destruction at its own hands."

"Could you explain this a little more?"

"Yes, Eva. You will understand this better as we move through the chambers. But the seeker must be willing. Earlier you asked God to show you the way and you showed a willingness to understand. However, right now the focus is on regaining your health and strengthening your spirit. There is nothing to fear. You are protected by your spiritual armor. We will proceed with the lessons, the tasks, and the learning as they come before us in their own time. What Einstein's formula means to you is that we are all creatures of light. We are 'frozen' light, or light slowed down to manifest in physical matter. We come from the light. The light does not originate in us."

He continued, "The process of learning continues eternally, even after the physical body has decayed. This world is in a constant state of becoming, growing, and evolving. But you will see for yourself soon enough. To answer your question, after you have learned the lessons in all seven chambers of the castle, you will carry them in your soul, in the vibratory shells that extend from your body, and act from those lessons for the rest of the time you live in the physical world. When you depart the earth plane, you will take that knowledge and your personality form with you through the outer three shells that extend from your physical body. This is eternal life as it is promised in the sacred scriptures. The lower three shells will dissipate along with your body as they will no longer be needed for your advancement. It will be like shedding your clothes."

"How many energy shells are there surrounding my body?"

"There are seven energy shells. The ones closest to your body are slower in vibration and as they extend out, become higher in vibration. Each one corresponds to an energy-type transformer in a particular area of the body. Some of you call them energy centers or chakras. These centers process information coming from the energy shells. Again, this energy is part of the Holy Spirit or divine force. This explains literally how God can be in you, of you, and everywhere else at the same time. The Eastern and Western world experience the same energy but simply call it by a different name."

"So which energy center does the red chamber correlate with?"

"The red chamber is associated with the shell closest to the body called the etheric body, an energy grid-like template that sends the energy to the DNA in your cells to carry out its tasks. It is like the computer of the DNA."

"That makes so much sense. It explains why human beings have the ability of clairvoyance – they get their information from actual energy sources that comprise their senses."

"Yes, it's just a matter of language, Eva. Different cultures, different disciplines call these ideas by different names. In the East or in the world of science they are able to discuss energy with a different vocabulary. We are one people, Eva. Some people have not been as receptive to this but receptivity is the way of Sophia. You will be meeting her soon. You have taken your time to listen, Eva, therefore I would like to bestow upon you the fruit of the spirit of the first chamber – that of patience. Now however, before we leave the room, I want to introduce you to a good friend of mine, Persephone."

A young maiden entered the room, a pretty girl with a sweet countenance. She extended her hand to Eva. "I'm Persephone. Welcome to the castle, Eva."

"Thank you very much. So nice to meet you. Are you *the* Persephone of ancient Greek myths and lore?"

"I am she. The red chamber is my home, my territory. I'd like to give you a few hints for navigating the room. As you probably recall, I am Persephone the Innocent, which is really blissful at times. But the pain comes when the knowledge arrives – as it always will. And knowledge invariably brings conflict and the inevitable descent into a dark place of the soul. But this chamber is necessary for the balance of all things, and ensures that you take your first step into balancing the external and internal, the masculine and feminine energies within you. This leads to deep wisdom and knowing.

"Very interesting. I can already see aspects of myself in what you've told me so far."

Persephone smiled. "And you will see more. For my energy is an integral part of the sacred feminine aspect of the psyche of every man and every woman. In ancient societies, we had ritual gatherings to act out, learn, and perceive the essential energy patterns of the psyche as they emerge and manifest. This exists no longer, and many cannot find their way to understanding and balance, which has had a very negative effect on the world. Your task is to remember and re-learn about these essential patterns – for your own healing and that of the world."

"I'm fascinated, Persephone. Tell me more about your energy."

"I tend to be introverted and can easily get lost in my own dream-like world. I also enjoy my senses as they are more heightened than most people around me. I spend much time daydreaming and seem to know things intuitively – like what people are thinking and what they're going to say next. I'm also very sensitive and prone to depression – I tend to withdraw into my own world. Now I know that if I don't keep the other six goddess archetypes strong within me, I could easily have a break with reality, especially since I enjoy living in a dream world. So I constantly work to keep those other goddesses active."

Intrigued, Eva said, "Tell me about the other goddesses."

"There are seven of us altogether. Three are relationship goddess archetypes – Persephone, the daughter and innocent; Demeter, the mother and goddess of agriculture; and Hera, goddess of marriage. Three are independent archetypes, sometimes called 'virgin' goddesses, as that aspect of the feminine energy remains whole and untouched by any other energy except God. These goddesses are Hestia, goddess of home and hearth; Athena, goddess of wisdom and crafts; and Artemis, goddess of the moon and hunt. Aphrodite is the goddess of love, combining the elements of both independent and relationship goddesses. It is important to revere and strengthen all of these energies to achieve a healthy balance within. You will need all of them in your journey through the interior castle."

"I can already see the areas I need work in. I can't wait to get started." Eva said, hungry to learn more.

Persephone laughed, touching Eva's arm affectionately. "You already have, Eva. Let me tell you a bit more about the goddesses that have been confined to the dungeons of the collective psyche. You will need all of their energies activated within you during your journey through the interior castle. Demeter, the proverbial earth mother and relationship archetype, is the goddess of the second chamber, the orange energy center. She's in charge of relationships and nurturing. Hestia, goddess of the hearth, keeps the sacred fire burning – at home, in the community, and within the soul. She is the goddess of the third chamber, the yellow energy center of the solar plexus. Hera is archetype of the fourth chamber, the green energy center or heart space. She is another relationship archetype, the commander-in-chief of marriage. Athena is the goddess archetype of wisdom and craft, in charge of the fifth chamber, the blue throat area, where you learn to trust your voice. Artemis resides in the sixth chamber, the purple energy center or the third eye. She is the energy of the moon and hunt, an independent goddess. Her strengths lie in her ability to focus on her goals. Finally in the seventh chamber, the crown room of the inner chamber of the bride and bridegroom, we find Aphrodite, who is independent and relationship oriented, and combines the best of all the goddess archetypes to form a powerful energy, presence, and ability to affect the world. She is the supreme goddess of love.

"You'll continue to learn and grow as you move through the castle. Now is the time for stillness and to quiet your mind of turbulence. Become comfortable with that silence deep within, the center of the wheel that does not move. It is now time to rejuvenate and nourish yourself."

Persephone reached over and kissed Eva lightly on the cheek. "I must go now, my time with you is up. Go forth and enjoy your castle journey. Be ye not afraid, for all of us will be with you every step of the way. Bless you." Persephone bowed slightly and glided from the room.

The Second Chamber

Orange chamber – abdominal energy center

"Such things as are hidden I learned and such as are plain; for Wisdom, the artificer of all, taught me. For in her is a spirit intelligent, holy, unique, Manifold, subtle, agile, clear, unstained, certain, Not baneful, loving the good, keen, unhampered, beneficent, kindly, Firm, secure, tranquil, all-powerful, all-seeing, And pervading all spirits, though they be intelligent, pure and very subtle.

For Wisdom is mobile beyond all motion, and she penetrates and pervades all things by reason of her purity. For she is an aura of the night of God and a pure effusion of the glory of the Almighty; therefore nought that is sullied enteres into her.

For she is the refulgence of eternal light, the spotless mirror of the power of God, the image of his goodness. And she, who is one, can do all things, and renews everything while herself perduring; And passing into holy souls age to age, she produces friends of God and prophets."

— *Wisdom 7:21-27* [6]

AFTER PARTAKING OF POMEGRANATES, rhubarb, and apples at the banquet table, the Knight led Eva to the second chamber, the orange energy center of the castle. She followed him up one flight of a winding stone staircase and into a beautiful tangerine area. They stood outside the threshold while a woman glided toward them, clothed in a flowing white gossamer robe, a glow radiating from flawless, translucent skin. Her eyes shone like emeralds and her bright smile exuded loving energy. Eva felt bathed in warmth by the very presence of this figure.

"Eva, meet Sophia," the Knight said. "Sophia is full of youthful energy yet carries the wisdom of a crone. She is full of love and nurturing, compassion, and beauty for all living things. She is of the earth and of the heavens. The world is in dire need of her energy now."

Sophia reached out and squeezed Eva's hand. "I've been anticipating our meeting for a long time."

The Knight said, "Sophia will assist you on your sojourn of the second chamber. You are in safe and capable hands. But before you go, here is your spiritual armor for the orange chamber, your *hands of prayer*. Simply don the soft leather gloves, then fold your hands together, say your prayer, and ask your question for entry into the room."

Eva followed the Knight's instructions, closing her eyes in prayerful meditation. The words popped into her mind before she even tried to think of a question. "What must I do to have grace?"

Immediately the thought came to her, "You already have it, my child. You only have to open to the grace energy that is already within you."

"Aha!" said Eva to herself. "This is real. All the spiritual studies I've done have covered this, but it all seemed so remote and ephemeral, something beyond what I could really experience. Now it is real. I'm feeling and experiencing it personally, not just saying the words."

Walking ahead, Sophia opened the heavy stone door and motioned for Eva to follow her in. The high-ceilinged chamber was expansive, with three walls covered in rust-colored leather and the other wall a sparkling citrine-crystal stone formation. Bookcases overflowed with massive leather-bound tomes. In one corner, a couple argued, voices raised, with no compromise in sight. As she watched, it seemed that both were intent on winning.

Sophia spoke. "Eva, this is the chamber of relationship, of one-on-one relationship with others, and most importantly, your relationship with family, neighbors, groups, and community. Relationship plays a very important role in our lives here on earth, being a fundamental part of our growth and evolution. We are here to live and work in community, to love thy neighbor as thy self. It is very important that we get it right. If we don't, we stay trapped in the same old patterns of relating that just don't work, and we run the risk of getting sick. Not just emotionally and psychologically sick, but spiritually and physically sick as well.

"As women, we have been taught that relationships are our domain of expertise, that it is our duty to see that they work and that everyone is happy.

The Second Chamber

As predominant carriers of the feminine energy, we do have the innate predisposition to be the leaders in this area. As leaders we have the responsibility to teach and most importantly, to speak our truth, even at the cost of making others uncomfortable.

"Because many women have been indoctrinated to be pleasers, we have often denied the part of ourselves that needs to take a stand, for ourselves and others who have been victimized. We have, too many times, turned our faces from this responsibility because of the great cost of 'losing' a person or position and the approval, money, status, and social position that go along with our association to this. When we refuse this responsibility to act in the name of goodness, to face the truth head on, no matter the consequences, we lose our power, our energy. The life force begins to leak out from our body, and we often become tired, depressed, and have a feeling of weakness. This feeling of weakness may manifest physically in lower back pain and problems in the lower abdominal energy area.

"We frequently find ourselves blaming others when we need to hold up a mirror and examine ourselves. We fall into the trap of looking to relationships with others to 'fill the gaping hole' within us, instead of doing the work of finding our own fulfillment, what we were put on earth to do, and sharing it with others via healthy relationships. That's why the energy of the second chamber, the chamber that corresponds to the lower back and abdominal area of your body, is called the energy pattern of the Orphan."

"What about male-female relationships?" Eva asked.

Sophia responded, "A person should not look to their partner for romance. Find the romance within yourself through your great creative reservoir and celebrate it with another. This is true romance. Contrary to what romance novels, films, and popular music purport, you cannot find romance in another person; you can only share the romance that is already in you with another. The idea that you find romance in another is called romantic projection, and is probably the greatest fallacy of all time, and has created an enormous amount of pain and family problems in your society. This erroneous notion keeps males and females partner-hopping for that elusive other, that 'soul mate' that can satisfy all their needs and cravings. Many people seem to have this weakness for seeking a partner for their identity.

"Romantic projection or that perfect soul mate that will satisfy all those things does not exist. There is no perfect partner and no one true soul mate. True romance in relationship can be fun and exciting just as in romantic projection. However, true romance will expand you tremendously and is truly a gift from God. If you are in a romantic relationship and do not acquire independence, the ability to open your heart and give of yourself, and skills of compromise and healthy conflict resolution, then the great bonding or the soulmate experience will not emerge. This is the result of romantic projection."

"What happens to people when they crave the 'high of romance' and keep trying to recapture it in relationships?" Eva asked, thinking of Paris and her escapades.

"They partner-hop for their own personal satisfaction. They are unable to open their hearts. Romantic projection and the excitement that ensues is all about the way this other person makes them feel, it is not necessarily about opening the heart to a true deep, energy-sharing relationship. However, romantic projection can lead to a true deep relationship in two psychologically mature people. If, however, one or both partners stay in a first stage of a romantic encounter and continue to romantically project upon their partner, their partner can end up feeling drained and depleted because there is no energy cycling back to nourish them. A needy partner 'sucks energy into the black hole' that never gets satiated.

"This is why the deadly sin of lust is the trap of the second chamber. Sexual energy is a powerful, wonderful force in human beings, a gift from our Creator that allows us to experience a slice of heaven on earth in a very intense, profound, beautiful manner. But those who are needy, undeveloped, and who experience a spiritual void are in danger of using this energy in an addictive fashion.

"Persons who feel uncontrollable lust need to develop themselves in many areas, particularly spiritual, to re-pattern their emotional world into a healthier place, to fill that void within. They need to take time out from failed relationships to spend their vital energy working on themselves, to establish a balanced flow of energy within."

The Knight stepped in, "Women and men alike have been taught not to trust their instincts. They've been taught to look to experts for all their answers."

Sophia added, "True. Embedded in authoritative learning has been the message not to trust the self, especially the right-brain domain of intuition, creativity, images, and feeling. This is the part of the brain that connects us to the high self. Only the left, logical, scientific, structural, and sequential aspect of the brain has been honored in your society, the masculine aspect of the brain. The right brain harnesses the energy of the spiritual, the intuitive, and of Sophia's feeling domain. Sophia needs her rightful place on the throne as well as the king, the left brain.

"Your society's ills are a collective soul problem. You are not living from a place of deep spirit. You are collectively living in the limited arena of the ego, a structure of the human psyche and an element of time. To live from the soul requires a commitment to the journey and a willingness to stay true to the spirit within.

"The soul is frequently dormant until attention is focused upon it and it is activated, nurtured, fed, and watered. The soul knows when we spend time and attention on it instead of the seemingly important worldly tasks. This time and attention provides the foundation for our individuation. Then, one day, we find ourselves living out of the energy of our self-awareness, and we become transformed, constantly in a state of being and becoming, much like the metamorphosis of a caterpillar to butterfly. Part of your task in the castle process, Eva, is to develop your soul for your own edification. Then you can take this energy back to the world, spreading it everywhere. This is everyone's task in soul development. When you are changed, the world will be transformed before you. When you discover and know that true authority is within you, a reflection of the God energy within, you can begin the most exciting journey known to man, the sojourn to the center of your soul."

"I need for you to tell me how to do this, step-by-step. If you don't mind, I'll take notes." Eva pulled a small notepad and pencil from her skirt pocket. "I seem to process things better when I write them down. What must I do to master the second chamber?"

"Meditate on the meaning and beauty of the room as opposed to being trapped in it. Know your place in your family, your place in the world, and appreciate the value and necessity of kindness, the fruit of the spirit of the orange chamber. Realize your personal relationship with God is possible. I bestow the gift of kindness upon you."

Eva looked to the side of the room and noticed the green haze forming again. The Knight chuckled.

"Eva, go ahead and learn from experience in the green haze again. You learn deeper lessons from experience, or re-experiencing from your memories."

Taking a deep breath, Eva said, "Okay, become."

In an instant, she was transported back in time to her college roommate's home. Rebecca had been Eva's best friend and fellow cheerleader. They'd been 'joined at the hip, always together. Eva watched the drama unfold as Rebecca tenderly lifted a Phi Beta Kappa Honors Certificate from a musty box in her attic. Eva watched as memories flooded back to Rebecca – her stint as All-American Cheerleader at their university, the Awards Ceremony prior to graduation, where she swept the awards and gave the keynote speech. Tears stung Rebecca's eyes as she felt the anticipation of a full life ahead of her, the awesome adventure, and opportunity to help people and make a difference in their lives. She knew that is what she'd been put on this earth to do.

The doorbell chimed, followed by an insistent knock. Rebecca sighed and put away her treasures. *It had to be Medella. She said she would be dropping by for a drink on the way home from her luncheon.* The knocking became more insistent, even as Rebecca's feet dragged to the door.

"Well, I thought maybe I was going to have to send out a posse for you." Medella chirped while checking her make-up in the entry-hall mirror."

"How was the luncheon?" Rebecca asked, skillfully diverting the conversation to safer territory.

"Perfectly divine." Medella oozed. "That Patricia Springer sure knows how to throw a brunch – and she's so young. Why, she had petit fours shaped and decorated to match every species of flower she has growing in her garden. Those are some skills that would behoove you to acquire, Rebecca."

"You mean throwing a luncheon or growing a garden?" Rebecca asked, trying very hard to keep the bitterness from infecting her tone.

"Both." replied Medella, her tone commanding with expectation. "You spend far too much time reading and studying about that psychological drivel that doesn't have a hell of a thing to do with the real world. All you need to worry about is taking care of your husband, your children, and maintaining an acceptable social schedule."

Bile rose in Rebecca's throat. "Which no doubt includes Patricia-Springer-style petit fours luncheons."

"Yes."

Rebecca's stomach clenched. It would serve nothing to try and explain why she longed to pursue her own deepest desires and continuing education. It was not about money, it was about personal fulfillment – and living her mission. As much as Rebecca loved her family and friends, and enjoyed doing for them, she also needed to quietly attend to her own inner needs. She knew she needed to attend to her mind, body, and spirit, or a part of her would wither and die on the vine.

"Oh." Medella declared, pointing to a piece of jewelry she wore. "I will give this to you when you cut your hair. Isn't it time for you to have a short cut? You would look so cute with a short sassy haircut."

Rebecca started to say, "No, thank you. I like my hair the way it is." She did not want to appear ungrateful – and the piece of jewelry *was* pretty. Eva watched as Rebecca reluctantly accepted it.

"Thank you, Medella. This is so generous of you. I'll make an appointment right now to get my hair cut."

Nausea overcame Eva as she watched her friend compromise herself. Knowing she was in the haze and feeling the pain from watching Rebecca make a choice which weakened her, Eva said, "Become." and was transported instantly back into the castle.

Sophia draped her arm around Eva. "See how easy it is to get pulled into the world? Rebecca felt anger at being dis-empowered, but did not speak her truth. How could Rebecca have been empowered in this situation and become stronger for the experience?"

Eva sighed, "For starters, Rebecca could have taken a stand with Medella on how she preferred to spend her time, how she liked to wear her hair, and not feel as though she needed to make excuses. If Rebecca asked me for advice, I would suggest she not accept the gift. The piece of jewelry was not a gift – it was an act of manipulation. If she had not accepted the gift, both the gift and the manipulation would still belong to Medella."

Sophia approved, "This is a wonderful lesson for Rebecca to realize the importance of her voice and that it is her responsibility to speak her truth. This is where silence or acting against your desire is slothful."

A question formed in Eva's mind, "What do most people want more than anything in the world?"

Sophia seemed to read her mind, for she smiled and answered, "I'll let Demeter, the great mother and goddess of the second chamber, answer that question for you. Eva, meet Demeter."

A lovely middle-aged woman walked into the room, taking Eva's hand. "Hello, Eva. I'm Demeter, the mother aspect of Sophia. I'm here to answer your question about what people want more than anything."

"It's a joy to meet you, Demeter. Thanks for coming in to answer my question."

"My pleasure, Eva. What people want, the root of every motive, every thought, every action is to love and be loved, to feel the freedom to live an authentic life. Sovereignty. It is in this second chamber that we can begin to hear

God whispering to us. It is the place where we can feel free to stop talking while in prayer, telling God what we need, and become receptive. The act of listening is a lost art. Instead, most people continue to ask of God, and prayer becomes a wish list of needs. In the dominator society you live in, people don't really hear what is directed to them because they are too busy formulating their next line of thoughts. The art of communication gets derailed when listening does not occur. When people deviate from this, and try to meet their needs according to what the world prescribes, they become susceptible to depression, burnout, and dependency. This causes them to manipulate others or become manipulated, not a healthy path to take and one that can be fatal to soul growth."

Sophia continued, "Exactly, Demeter. Feelings of inadequacy that so often surface in our ego-driven life are always challenged in our relationships with others. It is usually only in relationship that we have a head-on collision with ourselves – revealing our shadow, our weaknesses, and this gives us an opportunity for inner work. It indicates to us the soft areas we need to work on when feelings of possessiveness emerge in the heat of a relationship – jealousy, envy, a need to control, a need to be right. A spotlight is shone on a part of our psyche that is asking to be healed. We need to take a mirror, an examination tool, and a scalpel. We must acknowledge our weakness, pray, be silent, meditate, and resolve to heal what has been revealed to us."

The Knight jumped in, "The quality of our relationship with others is determined by the quality of the relationship we have with ourselves, and with God. Do we feel alive inside or are we dependent on our primary relationship to make us feel alive? The degree of intimacy you are capable of attaining with another person, or the lack of it, is a prime indicator of the health of your internal world. Most people abhor being alone, but it is in the aloneness that you face your deepest fears and experience personal growth. It is here that the unconscious mind makes itself known to the ego. There is no substitute or short-cut for spending quality time alone with the divine energy."

Demeter added, "Organs of the body that correlate with the second chamber include the sexual organs, bowels, organs and muscular-skeletal structures in and around your hips. Excessive energy trapped in the second chamber can manifest in sexual dysfunction and addiction. Energy leaks from the room can manifest in inhibited sexual desire, frigidity, and impotence."

Eva asked, "What about mental and emotional issues?"

The Knight answered, "Those issues may include financial and sexual concerns, power and control, creativity, ethics, and honor in relationship to others.

The Second Chamber

Most illnesses here result from fear of losing control. Also prevalent among women particularly is 'the bag-lady syndrome,' the fear of being unable to take care of themselves financially. With a balance and flow of energy through the second chamber, women will feel confident in the ability to take care of themselves and take appropriate risks to move forward guided by their high self, or soul, that aspect of spirit that is connected with God."

"That sheds light on much that is often confusing." Eva exclaimed.

At this point, Sophia and Demeter guided Eva through the labyrinth of the room. "Deep-seated emotional issues of the orange chamber are those of betrayal, financial loss, poverty, abandonment, and isolation. When we are balanced and healthy in the second chamber, we naturally form relationships with people who support our personal path and growth and remove ourselves or avoid relationships which stunt our growth and drain our energy."

The Knight stepped in behind them. "Be careful that in all your relationships there is a balanced exchange of energy. Pay attention to your energy field when you are around others. When the energy you release is absorbed up, you are in contact with a person whose energy is negative, unhealthy, literally circulating in the wrong direction, taking on a vacuum-type force. You will feel drained and exhausted physically.

"A healthy relationship allows for a nurturing, flowing exchange of energy that makes you both feel expanded. In a deeper relationship, you intertwine soul strands with those whom you trust implicitly, those who would not violate your spirit. Your heart is revealed by your actions."

When they reached the end of the labyrinth Sophia and Demeter scrolled out a papyrus, which gave the Four Essential Truths of Life. Those truths require you to be in the moment, to act from your center, and be who you are. Be aware of what resonates in your soul, for this is what compels you. Speak and act from your truth and receptivity, practicing discernment without judging. Look to God.

Eva held the papyrus close and examined the four truths inscribed:

1. Be in the moment through ceaseless prayer, silence and contemplation.
2. Stay aware of your essence, operating from your core of truth at all times.
3. Act with discernment through prayer for God's will in your life choices.
4. Walk with faith and courage for positive change resulting through action in the world.

The Third Chamber

Yellow chamber – solar plexus energy center

"My fruit is better than gold, yes, than pure gold,
and my revenue than choice silver.
On the way of duty I walk, along the paths of justice,
Granting wealth to those who love me, and filling their
treasuries."

— *Proverbs 8:19-21* [7]

EVA BASKED in the warm amber-yellow light of the third chamber of the castle. The Knight took his place beside her, his hands folded. The energy crackled the air around them as the Knight bowed his head, then handed Eva the spiritual armor of the yellow chamber.

"This is the *shield of faith*, my child. Wear it to extinguish the flaming arrows of negative energy. The third chamber of the castle corresponds with the solar plexus area of your body, the very center of your being. The energy patterns of this chamber deal with personal power and your very purpose here on earth. The deadly sin of this place, the one that every human being grapples with on some level, is unresolved anger. If anger is not resolved, addressed, worked through, then released, it will weigh you down and pull you away from your essence, and true mission on earth.

Sophia interjected, "The major battle fought by the energy pattern of the internal warrior, residing in the solar plexus, is that between the lower self, the ego, and the soul. The mistake most humans make is that they never break through the barriers of this necessary but limited psychological structure of the personal ego. The ego holds an important function of our psyche during our sojourn on this planet. The ego is good. It is used to develop social skills and negotiate our way through the world of relationships. Just as your body allows you to have a physical experience in the world, your ego is the core of your personality and allows you to have emotional and mental connections in the world. The problem arises when people continue to operate solely out of this limited structure that is only concerned with the expansion of itself.

"The task and challenge for us as human beings is to break out of the ego in trust that there is something deeper and more universal than the ego's limited framework of its narrow purpose. This leap of faith cracks the ego's shell open, like a cocoon cracking open for a butterfly to emerge, allowing infinite development. Your task, Eva, is to take the leap of faith, and allow your ego to serve your soul and God, so that you may live a life of peace, contentment, and fulfillment."

"Become." Eva closed her eyes and whispered, knowing it was time to experience the lesson of the third chamber. Opening her eyes, she sat next to Paris, along with a room full of people. There were balloons, gifts, food, and drinks for all. Everyone began to sing "Happy Birthday" to their dear friend Carol. Laughter filled the air as the volume in the room rose. Carol was opening the last of her many gifts, a beautiful designer dress. However, the dress appeared a bit large for her slight build. Paris watched over her shoulder as she read the gift certificate included in the card. Paris looked puzzled and her expression soon changed to dismay. The gift certificate was for breast augmentation by a local plastic surgeon.

Eva watched as Carol quietly closed the card but sweetly thanked the giver. She then discreetly walked toward the kitchen in an attempt to disappear but Paris waltzed close behind.

"What was that I saw in your card? Do you want to talk about this?" Paris chirped.

Carol responded with a troubled look but maintained her composure, "Oh, it's nothing, that is, nothing I will accept. Besides, I'd really rather not discuss it."

Eva witnessed all she cared to see and closed her eyes to return.

Stepping out of the haze, Eva exclaimed, "I see the error of standard ways, the product of a society that places more emphasis on physical beauty than the soul. When Chris and I were first married, many of my friends were having plastic surgery to improve their bodies in various ways. I remember the day I told Chris that changing my body was not an option for me. Chris wrapped his arms around me and told me that he hadn't married me for the size of my breasts – he married me for my heart. I was also grateful for his acceptance of me just as I am, as well as his affirmation of my choice. Now if someone delivered such a 'gift' to me unsolicited, I would look at them with sadness, realizing it speaks more about their own unfulfilled needs and was not meant to harm. Some people judge themselves against worldly standards and try to perfect their own naturally imperfect image. This strive for perfection can be fruitless, a task without end. I pray they find self-love and can realize God loves them just as they are.

"Sophia, is it possible that woman of all ages are trying to connect to the sacred feminine by symbolically enhancing themselves with physical changes and adornments?" Eva questioned.

"In your world, women have not been given role models or icons for the sacred feminine. Each of us will unconsciously live out what our soul needs, to grow closer to the source." Sophia explains.

"Now it is time for your introduction to Hestia, goddess of the hearth and keeper of the feminine energy of the third chamber. She may be able to answer your question also." Sophia continued.

A radiant beauty with a nimbus of golden hair stepped in from the great hallway. Eva took her hand, "You must be Hestia. I'm Eva. Welcome."

Hestia smiled, her eyes radiating depth, "The third chamber is a wonderful place to be, Eva. The fire is always burning in the center, just as the flame burns in the center of your soul. The fire not only represents your passion, but the intuitive side of yourself, that inner sanctuary. It is where you find a deep commitment to yourself and your purpose in this world. It is where you enjoy solitude, the pleasure of your own company, and it is where you start the journey of spiritual meeting – where your worldly self meets your soul in the presence of God. If the development of the yellow chamber is ignored, emotional distance and dissonance sets in, and an anti-social stance occurs. This can be detrimental to your growth. Let your solitude work toward a greater connection with yourself, allowing a deeper connection to the earth, other people, and the Creator."

"Thank you for your clear guidance." said Eva.

The Knight continued, "Many people who lose energy from the solar plexus energy center of the body become chronically angry, controlling, distrustful, judgmental, lonely, and addiction-prone. The power of the spiritual warrior comes from an inner strength, a knowing that his/her guidance flows from a divine, universal force rather than the human, limited energy system."

The Knight said, "The task of the third chamber is difficult but the results are worthwhile. Successful mastery results in a focused life and effectiveness in this world, which leads to positive self-regard and faith, which springs from courage. A warrior needs these strengths to take the risks necessary to fulfill a higher purpose, that of self-development for the betterment of the individual and the world. The fruit of the spirit is discipline as opposed to the ego's insistence on instant gratification."

Eva conjectured, "It seems that part of the ego's job is to protect the vulnerable part of the person. How can one successfully bring down those walls without harming the vulnerable, still undeveloped part of us that needs that protection?"

The Knight answered, "The vulnerable or innocent child within is that aspect of ourselves that trusts unconditionally. The ego, in contrast, has a strong need to protect the vulnerable psyche against any outside force – and that includes change and transformation. It also stays clear of the unconscious, and would rather stay in the safe territory of the conscious mind. The ego seeks to preserve itself by remaining in the safety of sameness, of what is familiar.

"The first task is to meditate, prayerfully expressing the desire for your personal spirit to develop beyond the confines of the ego, while embracing the vulnerable aspect of the self. The second task is, while meditating, to observe the ego at play. Recognize it, without judgment or attachment, when the ego is taking the stage. Love the ego, for it is a vital part of you, but learn to recognize when the ego is driving you, and gently ask it to take a back seat.

"The third task is to embrace the ego and recognize it for what it is, a necessary construct to maneuver us through life on this earth. Look at it not as an enemy but as a very protective big brother or big sister. The ego is just doing its job, even though it gets in the way of our growth at times.

"The fourth task is to have a dialogue with the ego from the spiritual side of the self. Allow your ego to dance and frolic at times. It needs fresh air, sunshine, and fun, too. The ego is not only necessary but adds flavor to this life. But the ego is limited to this world, to this body. The psychological structure of the ego does not remain with us when we die, as the energy patterns of the soul, that of the fourth, fifth, sixth, and seventh energy centers do. Learn to recognize when you are living a life to serve the ego as opposed to living a life that is serving the soul. The fruits of your spiritual work will travel with you when you die to this world, and die from your fleshly body. The fruits of the ego go the way of the flesh when you die."

Sophia stepped forward, "The fruit of the spirit of the third chamber, that of discipline, is bestowed on you now, Eva. Now we are ready to go to the banquet table and replenish before we go to the great and most important fourth chamber, the energy center of the heart."

The Fourth Chamber

Green chamber – heart energy center

"Mine are counsel and advice;
mine is strength; I am understanding.
By me kings reign, and lawgivers establish justice;
By me princes govern, and nobles;
all the rulers of earth.
Those who love me I also love,
and those who seek me find me."

— Proverbs 8:14-17 [8]

SOPHIA, dressed in a flowing emerald-colored robe she had donned following the banquet, led Eva to the fourth chamber, the green chamber of the castle, tucked into the very heart of the fourth level. "Eva, this chamber holds the most important and powerful energy of the universe, the energy of love."

So stunning was this green area that it took Eva's breath away. Waterfalls trickled down green granite rock walls and lush vegetation surrounded them. The room pulsated with life. Breathing the air felt fresh and invigorating.

Sophia continued, "Love is the uniting energy of the universe, the be all and end all. It is the energetic glue that holds everything in unity and is necessary for anything to exist as a whole. Love flows into and emanates from the heart region of your body."

Sophia placed a hand over her heart and smiled. "The heart harbors an intelligence of its own, which communicates directly with the mind."

The Knight walked in with the spiritual armor for the fourth room. "Eva, here is your *breastplate of righteousness*. Wear it at all times for spiritual protection, and so your actions in this world will always be aligned with your heart."

Sophia helped Eva adjust the breastplate over her chest. Eva immediately felt the spiritual protection of the shield and the warmth of love pouring into her from the Knight and Sophia.

The Knight stepped up, his own armor shining. "I must warn you of the deadly sin of the fourth chamber before we go in any further. That sin is gluttony. Like greed and envy, gluttony is the perpetual consumption of energy in an effort to fill the black hole, or spiritual void within. If those people who experience a need to overindulge in eating or any other activity have fallen into the deadly sin of gluttony, it is a sign that they need to stop, take heed, and do their inner work. All of the deadly sins are metaphors, a warning to inform you that you have spiritual work to be done so that you can bring yourself back into balance, harmony, and wholeness. Your task is to recognize it, meditate and pray, and use the clear space to structure new patterns when the old ways of sin break apart, to structure new balanced patterns that transform the old dissonant patterns of sin."

Eva replied, "Are you saying that we are not doomed to hell and damnation when we fall into sin?"

With Knightly conviction, he replied, "No, the sin is there for you to learn and grow from, to recognize it, acknowledge the act of deviation from the path, to purge it, and move forward. Guilt serves as a warning bell that a heartfelt confession is needed. But once it has gotten your attention to take action for change, it must be released. Unresolved guilt binds up your energy, and a reservoir of shame builds up. We are all on the same journey, and we all stumble. It is not what we've done or not done to sin that builds or diminishes character. But it is our willingness and ability to confess, forgive ourselves and others, and move forward on our path with courage and intent for goodness that defines character."

Sophia added, "When our energy centers close down, usually because of fear, the energy flowing through our heart area is greatly diminished and our life force is minimized. Life energy does not adequately nourish the cells, tissues, and organs of our body, and we fall into 'energy starvation' because our body is cut off from its life force. If we open our hearts, the universal energy, Holy Spirit, or *chi* flows in and we are nourished by it. This is the concept of the living Christ, the energy that stays with us and is available to us at all times. Hera, goddess of the fourth room, and great wife, is here to tell you more about this concept."

Hera walked in and greeted everyone. "Eva, welcome. There are three important concepts we must learn in order to open the isolation of a fearful, closed heart. The first important truth is that separateness is an illusion. Everything is made up of swirling energy, and energy fields flow together in a constant interaction. If we had the vision to detect energy fields, we would not see the separateness that our eyes behold. We would perceive a blending and sharing of all. That is the ultimate reality. To live in this world and fulfill our task of spiritual development, we must not see things separately. The heart learns through its soul work that the separateness we see with our physical eyes is only a product of our temporal existence. In eternal existence there is no separation, although each energy pattern of a person is an entity in and of itself, as unique as each snowflake, and will remain so throughout eternity.

"The second important concept in opening your heart is that since sharing and exchange of energy in relationship is so important to emotional, mental, and physical health, do not be afraid to touch others, and spread the energy of love, for it will return to you in abundance. Finally, we must give of ourselves freely from the source of goodness. If we appear to give of ourselves for reasons that will give us status with others, the source is not organic and the flow of energy will not be healthy. One must become prayerful and meditate in this area. It is better not to give than to give begrudgingly or for an ulterior motive.

"The quality of energy that is sent out, whether it is positive or negative, will return to its source with a ten-fold increase in energy. Like a boomerang, it gains momentum and speed. Negative thoughts will come back to the sender with increased intensity, hitting much harder the person who sent the negative energy force than the person who received it. This is an example of divine justice."

Sophia walked to the waterfall, a soft breeze lifting her fine hair. "When we hit the wall," she said, placing her hand against the emerald-colored granite, "we are in a dark night of the soul and it feels that we will never see the light of day again. But the next dawn will be the brightest. It is through the black abyss that transformation occurs and we no longer see through a glass darkly. When we enter the dark night of the soul, the dungeon of the castle, it helps to know that it is just one step in the alchemical process of glorious soul work.

"Working through your soul's wounds helps you connect with the soul and others profoundly, and persons who have grown up in a sheltered environment are probably more handicapped and wounded than those who grew up in a dysfunctional family. They think the world owes them comfort and they have not developed the emotional musculature to withstand the slings and arrows of malevolent forces in the world they will eventually encounter. Any person who refuses reflection ends up leading a shallow life, a life of quiet desperation. Being with friends and loved ones is paramount to nourishing your heart center."

Eva questioned, "But so many times I feel an iron vise around my heart, to the point I can't breathe, much less think about love energy."

The Fourth Chamber

Sophia smiled, "This is where courage comes in, courage to forge ahead in spite of the iron grip of fear around your chest. Taking action breaks the hold of the grip, loosening it, and allowing it to fall to the ground. Fear is a very strong force, but courage, faith, and love are so much stronger. Action, honesty, and truth strengthen character and soul."

The Knight added, "The fourth chamber is the most essential place for your physical survival in this world. For your body to function properly, your heart and circulatory system must work optimally. In your world we see heart attacks as the number-one killer. Emotional and spiritual issues that may occur prior to these physical manifestations could be fear, resentment, residual guilt, lack of forgiveness, lack of compassion, jealousy, hatred of self, distrust of self, lack of hope, self-centeredness, or ego-driven narcissism. This is how the soul speaks directly to the body. Some people have learned this art of healing and understand the mind-body-spirit connection. This is why we speak of someone being healed, not cured. They may still have the physical condition or dis-ease but they have come to terms with the pain or illness on a mental, emotional, and spiritual level."

Eva stepped forward, uttering the word "Become." Shrouded in the green haze, she watched her neighbor, Jane, as she held her screaming newborn son in her arms while attempting to console her two-year-old daughter. Jane sighed in frustration and exhaustion. There didn't seem to be enough of her to go around. With her free hand, she punched in the numbers of her husband Gary's cell phone. She knew exactly where he'd be – at happy hour, his nightly escape from reality and responsibility.

A whiskey-laden voice slurred a "Hello" from the other end of the line. Jane abruptly asked to speak to her husband. Jane heard a muffled version of, "The witch is after you with her broomstick." Laughter in the background only served to fuel her escalating anger.

"Yeah." said Gary, his tone betraying the annoyance he felt at the sobering interruption of the daily happy hour at the revolving-door bar of another friend's home.

"Gary, I need you here. I only have two arms and four kids. Please come home. Now."

Gary emitted a disgusted sigh and hung up abruptly. Eva could tell that Jane's frustration quickly escalated to humiliation and anger. By the time Gary reached the door, Jane was seething with rage.

Jane yelled, "I've had enough of your self-centered, alcohol-centered lifestyle. It's time you take some responsibility around here and help me with *our* children. I can't do this by myself. I am not a one-woman show."

Gary shot back, "And I work hard all day to support you and the children. I need to decompress after a stressful day and I'll be damned if I'm going to be deprived of happy hour with my friends."

"How are you going to feel when I deprive you of your children by taking them and leaving? I cannot do this anymore."

Red-faced, Gary turned on his heels and stormed out the door, slamming it hard behind him.

After saying "Become" Eva watched from outside the haze, taking an objective view. Now she could see that anger and judgment had clouded her neighbor's motivation – to create a relationship that served as a foundation for their family and home – a center point of safety. What Jane could have communicated to Gary was that because she loved him and their children so deeply, she needed him to step up to the plate with her and be her partner in life. He needed to hear that she'd married him for his heart, and loved and accepted him as he was. In turn, she needed to feel his strength, his commitment, and love in action – by putting the family first. Only then could their relationship deepen, blossom, and grow in God's love – as they moved toward the divine relationship that God intended for a man and wife.

"I'm pulling for Gary to see the benefit of his choice to be home with his family. I guess some men would make the choice to stay with their friends." said Eva. "The first-step nudge back to marriage and family happens with one person returning to love."

Sophia said, "The most common stumbling block in the fourth chamber is lack of forgiveness, of yourself for the wrongs you have done to others and done to yourself, and the wrongs others have done to you. However, forgiveness does not require 'letting others off the hook' or saying what they did was okay. I quote Galations 6:7-8[9]: 'Make no mistake: God is not mocked, for a person will reap only what he sows, because the one who sows for his flesh will reap corruption from the flesh, but the one who sows for the spirit will reap eternal life from the spirit.' Forgiveness means releasing the dead wood from your system so the negative feelings no longer have an adverse effect on your energy. Forgiveness means no longer being the victim. And with the release, you become healed."

Eva said, "Aha. I actually felt the release in me, like a pop. I've just experienced forgiveness – I have forgiven the past wounds. I feel light, free at last of the burdens. Now I'm aware of how I used the pain to grow and transform. I would not be standing here in the fourth chamber with you now if my body hadn't shut down. Now I feel like I can go out and run a marathon."

Sophia laughed, her face radiant. "And you are. The work you're doing now is equivalent to running a super-marathon. This is the hardest work you will ever do, Eva. It is also the most worthwhile work you will ever do. You are living on a much higher spiritual plane now. Therefore stay in this higher altitude of appreciation and gratitude and lift up your heart."

The Knight added, "Jesus asked that we leave the dead and get on with life. Eva, you have left the dead behind – baggage from the past and parts of yourself that have died, to make room for new parts of yourself. This is what transformation calls for."

Sophia bowed her head in prayer. "We listen and hear the voice of our hearts. We receive, then give back in a continual flow. Stay in your heart, Eva. Let all your actions spring from your center of love, joy, and kindness. Nurture your sense of wonder, and revere the *mystery*."

The Fifth Chamber

Blue chamber – throat energy center

"Jesus then said to those Jews who believed in him,
'If you remain in my word, you will truly be my disciples,
and you will know the truth, and the truth will set you free.'"

— John 8:31-32 [10]

BEFORE ENTERING the dazzling blue chamber, Eva asked the question, "How can I bring my personal will into conformity with the will of God?"

Listening had become natural because Eva is now able to hear the silent words that formed eloquently in her mind, "By being resolute in your practice of prayer and meditation. It is only by quieting the mind that you will be able to discern the deep, subtle voice of intuition guiding you through the labyrinth of your high self. Aligning your will with the Creator's will is the greatest challenge of the spiritual journey. The more you practice it, the more natural and habitual it becomes. Then you dwell in a state of natural meditation all your waking moments. You have learned and cultivated the art of living in your center, living a meditative life. However, it is important not to despair when you are pulled away from the main path. The path to goodness is always there, and you will not lose your way back to it.

"You will know you are on the path by the fruits you bear. The important thing is to recognize when you fall. You can use the experience of pain at having disconnected with the soul, and recognize that you want to be back in communion with God. It is much too painful for you to be separated from God after you have experienced the bliss of re-connection. We can never find this peace in another person, as much as we try. When we attempt to find this peace or joy in another, it sets the stage for addictive relationships and distracts us from God. Unless you find this peace, contentment, and joy in your own castle, you will not find it in another. You can only share it with another."

The Fifth Chamber

Both the Knight and Sophia extended their hands to Eva as she entered the blue pulsating arena of the fifth chamber. Surrounded by the azure blue of the sky, Eva felt high above the earth.

"You have just entered the blue chamber of the castle, which corresponds to the throat energy center of your body. The altitude is higher in this spiritual arena, and the air is thinner. Be careful to breathe deliberately and deeply. With the green chamber as a bridge between the lower three physical centers, the first, second, and third chambers, the fifth chamber leads the way into the pure spiritual rooms."

The Knight handed her a *braided leather belt* with the word "Truth" embossed on the front, containing shiny pellets of mercury. "This is the chamber where truth becomes essential. It is the area of communication and will. It is the chamber where the primary task is that of discernment. The fifth chamber is the most difficult to master as it requires looking at yourself in the mirror to see your truth, and having the courage to report the truth back to your inner self. This very important step on the soul journey cannot be skipped or omitted. You cannot see the truth in others or in the world until you see it in yourself."

Eva took a deep breath and closed her eyes in meditation. Sophia stepped in beside her and placed a loving arm on her shoulder. "There is nothing to be afraid of, my child, for we are with you and support you."

Sophia seemed to tune into Eva's thoughts as words from the sacred text suddenly flowed through her mind, "Know the truth, and the truth shall set you free."

The Knight spoke, "Discerning the Creator's will is the greatest challenge of all. And it means finding your voice to creatively express your will, and that of truth. This can be done in many ways: through speech, poetry, song, and all creative expressions."

Still in a state of receptivity, words again passed through Eva's mind quickly, remembering she had heard this before "When your will is in Thy will, you will have peace."

Sophia added softly, "When uncertainty pulls at you, remember the words you have just heard. Then you will know. If you do not feel the smooth flowing river of peaceful energy within, if rapids and undercurrents force their way into your being, you are not in the will of God, and you will not feel peace. You are most likely still operating in the limited realm of the ego. The biggest challenge of the spiritual journey, and one of the most difficult tasks for any human to undertake, is harnessing the power to speak, act out of truth and confession, and be willing to acknowledge the shadow within because it is so inordinately painful. It is the slippery precipice where many turn back out of fear."

Eva closed her eyes, and found her voice to speak the word "Become." and enter the green haze once again. This time she watched with a heavy heart as her sister's husband played racquetball with another beautiful woman. Eva had known for awhile that Matt had not been present when she was with her sister, Christina. He always seemed to have something else to do. Her gut told her there was a problem, but she hadn't known what it might be – until now.

Eva continued to watch as Matt returned home late for supper. Christina confronted Matt and asked him to explain why he was consistently late. His explanation did not satisfy Christina and she told him her suspicions. He vehemently denied any wrongdoing or sexual involvement, but Eva saw that Christina's heart believed differently. Christina told Matt that the constant pain in her heart became an intuitive reminder that could not be assuaged with objective, rational thought. Christina continued to share her beliefs and intuitions that if her husband was not physically involved with another woman, then he was emotionally involved. She explained to Matt that by spending valuable time with the other woman, time which could be spent with Christina, his energy was being diverted from their marriage and family to another person – the hurt felt like as much a violation as any sexual encounter could have been.

Eva watched as Christina paid a visit to the other woman, telling her that her marriage and family are important to her and she needed her help to save them. Christina gave her the benefit of the doubt and spoke to the other woman's conscience. Then Eva watched Christina ask Matt to spend more time with her and their children, and to work on their marriage together. She asked that they listen to each other with heartfelt discussions and open and honest communication. Christina expressed her feelings to Matt about her pain and loneliness at his "absence." Miraculously, the experience helped them become closer as a couple and a family.

Returning from the haze, Eva recognized the strength in Christina's approach. She always knew her sister was of strong character but this proved her strength in action. Eva now understood the value in discerning truth, finding voice, and taking action. The choice empowered Christina, increasing her internal fortitude and spiritual foundation. Eva was able to see how honest communication begins the healing process and that this difficult time presented itself as a painful but wonderful opportunity for her sister's marriage to grow. The scripture "in all circumstances give thanks"[11] came to mind as Eva realized how Christina was able to faithfully live through the difficulty.

Walking to the door, Sophia said, "Now Eva, I'd like for you to meet Athena, goddess of wisdom."

Athena flowed through the door, dressed in a dazzling cobalt-blue gown, her dark hair piled high on her head. Eva took her hand and greeted her.

Athena, goddess of the fifth chamber, of intellect, wisdom, and craft jumped into the conversation as if she'd been there the whole time. "So good to meet you, Eva. In reference to the self, most people, when they come face to face with their own monsters, turn around and run, or build up an arsenal of defenses to use as a shield. But it does not reduce the pain. On some level, they always live with it and carry the baggage. It takes massive amounts of energy to uphold the emotional fortress that protects the shadow. But I am with you every step of the way to support and nurture you, to hold you, and wipe your tears when the pain seems too much to bear. The Knight, the masculine face of God, lifts you up and protects you, allowing me to embrace and nourish you. Then you can purge yourself of the old baggage, the dead wood of pain you have been holding onto for so long, and allow space for the new hope and positive, constructive energy. In the fifth chamber, the most difficult room to master, you will learn to think well on your feet, you will speak the truth as you believe it to be, solve practical problems, and form strategic alliances with your male energy. If this process is circumvented, it could lead to emotional distancing, disconnection, craftiness, and lack of empathy for others."

The Knight warned, "Many who try to skip this step attempt to do so by using spirituality as a balm, to make them feel better without doing the gritty work inside themselves. It simply does not work. The balm of the spirit may also come in the form of alcohol, food, tobacco, drugs, promiscuous sex, obsessions, over-work, or frenetic busyness. Addictions are prominent in the fifth chamber as any addiction is a way to avoid the pain of the truth."

Sophia linked her arm in Eva's, stepping deeper into the royal-blue atmosphere. "Negative actions resulting from choices made from the ego, without the awareness, prayer, meditation, purging, and discernment of the high self causes 'energy leaks,' which weaken the body, mind, and spirit. If you do not practice these things, and choose to ignore the body's signals – the clenching of the stomach, the heaviness in the chest, neck, throat, and digestive problems – then you will only spiral deeper into negativity and suffer more energy loss. It will affect the energy center of the organ in which that particular task is associated."

Eva said, "Like when we tell a lie, our throat may constrict and our voice sometimes sounds thready."

Sophia answered, "Exactly. Your body does not lie, even if your ego does."

The Knight said, "Now it is time for you to be rewarded for your work of the fifth chamber. Faith is a state of being and the fruit of the spirit that sets, balances, and charges the energy of the body into a healthy, healing state. Faith integrates the psychological components of the personality with spiritual components and integrates them. Faith allows you the freedom to live your truth. Choices made in faith have God's truth, the full support and power of the universe behind them. Faith the size of a mustard seed can literally move mountains or split the sea."

Sophia said, "Conversely, any choice made from fear violates the pure spiritual energy of faith, and the faith recedes from the fear. This leaves you with the fear. The origin of negative actions, negative thoughts, and negative deeds is fear. Fear is a false god that keeps us imprisoned. When we are motivated by fear, we are vulnerable to becoming addicted to many false gods – money, power, and promiscuous, self-serving sexual encounters. These actions are a way of escaping, avoiding, and rejecting the spiritual side of life, and never lead to fulfillment. When we are seduced by anything, we relinquish control and become victims.

"Gossip and manipulation are birthed in fear. They are violations of other human beings. Rape is also an act of violation and does not occur just on the physical level. One human being can rape another's energy field with verbal abuse or violent, dis-empowering words and thoughts. One can kill the spirit. When Jesus spoke the words 'You shall not kill,'[12] he wasn't just referring to the killing of the body. He also meant the spirit.

"Rape and spirit killing spring from the egoistic need to dominate and control. These negative actions poison the energy system and produce destructive actions. Organic, universal justice will always prevail. Justice is always served at the energy level whether we ever see it manifest materially or not. With every choice you make in the world, ask yourself if this choice is based on faith or if this choice is based on fear. Then go into a prayerful, meditative state. You will then know the answer. Listen to your body, hear your inner voice, and listen to the soft hush of the voice of God. It will tell you the truth."

Sophia continued, "If you'd like, we can replenish our bodies at the banquet table. Then we will be prepared to experience the sixth chamber."

The Sixth Chamber

Purple chamber – third eye energy center

"Her fetters will be your throne of majesty;
her bonds, your purple cord."

— Sirach 6:30 [13]

SOPHIA walked with Eva through the long corridor and up the winding stone steps to the sixth chamber, located in a tower overlooking miles of azure-blue sky and a glorious purple mountain range peaked with snow. Shimmering amethyst crystals covered the walls, which seemed to pulsate with a life and intelligence all their own. Eva felt God's love resonating within her and a sense of peace pervaded within. The Knight stood quietly in the far corner, his eyes closed, head bowed, and hands folded in earnest, solemn prayer.

Sophia spoke softly, observing the pristine reverence of the high room. Rich, purple-toned velvet drapes hung from the long windows, framing the breathtaking scenery in a handsome portrait. The air smelled clean, pure, making Eva want to drink in the oxygen, pushing it to the bottom of her lungs. The pristine light seemed to cast a magical spell on every object on the horizon and in the room.

The Knight raised his head, opened his eyes and smiled gently. "You are getting closer to the seventh chamber, Eva, and the air is even thinner up here. You must take care to breathe deeply and focus intently as you have learned so well from the lower rooms."

Eva nodded in understanding, a feeling of anticipation and excitement flooding over her. She could feel a shift into a greater level of awareness just by being in the sixth chamber of the castle. She no longer felt fear and apprehension, only trust as her experiences came together to form a greater understanding of her life and why things happened as they did.

The Knight stepped up, "Here is your spiritual armor for this chamber, my child."

He handed her a sword clothed in a scabbard. "Wear the *sword of the spirit in its scabbard* and hold it close to you for safety. With it you will discern the true nature of the world. The double-edged sword represents the left eye of the masculine and the right eye of the feminine. The point of the sword is the third eye, or the true picture, which blends both of the visions of right and left. The third eye is the eye of deep wisdom, and noetic or spiritual intuition, a knowing of the soul, which sees everything as a whole. As we transform energies, the gut-level intuition of the third chamber moves to the sixth chamber. It then becomes real, intuitive knowing. With the whole picture comes peace, a peace that surpasses all understanding from the point of view of the rational left-brain intellect. The third eye vision goes beyond belief into fundamental knowing, that your spirit is part of God's spirit. Trust becomes a part of the essence of your being, and the act of moving forward is done with ease, knowing that every life experience that comes onto the path is one that is needed for advancement of the soul and is part of the higher good. For everything we are to be grateful."

Sophia stepped up, "Eva, you may ask your question now for entry into the chamber."

Eva bowed her head in meditation and waited for the question to emerge from her center. "From which eyes do I search for the truth?"

Suddenly Eva noticed a mirror on the opposite side of the chamber. When she looked at her image she saw a swirling rainbow of energy swiftly moving around her body, almost like a beautiful light show. The colored bands wove in and out, giving the light strands a braid-like appearance. The layer of light closest to her body appeared as a reddish color and the darkest of the energies. The second layer was an orange shade blended with the subtler yellow layer. Beyond the yellow pulsated a lovely emerald-green. The green bled into the cobalt blue, which segued into purple. Encircling the rainbow of colors was a brilliant white, rimmed in gold. Eva blinked her eyes in an attempt to capture the image, but it was ever changing, like a kaleidoscope. Eva noticed layers of color were the exact arrangement of the colors in a rainbow – our body's energies are a rainbow!

An insight bubbled up within her: This is who we are – holy spirit, *prana, chi,* energy fields that interact with everything else in the universe – even thought forms that are thousands, even million miles away. Eva closed her eyes to meditate on this astounding revelation, allowing the profundity of it to permeate her entire being. When she opened her eyes and looked again into the mirror, everything in the room, inanimate and animate objects alike, were no longer objects but lumps of this rainbow of light, all blending together for an amazing elaborate display of color and light, ever moving, ever changing.

Incredulous, Eva stole her eyes from the image, looking at the Knight, once again seeing him in solid form rather than pulsating light. "I really see how things work from the inside out," she said. "This explains why I seem to know certain things in my intuitive self that I could not possibly know without the information being relayed to me. Thoughts have energy. I can see them coming from the head into the field and merging with the colored streamers around the body. Thought comes in first, then becomes emotion, reflected in the colored streamers. Thoughts become part of your physical make-up and bodily intelligence by traveling through the energy field, a form of spiritual DNA, a re-membering, a built-in knowing, a 'wisdom of the ages' that has, during this life, been covered over by conditioning and indoctrination."

Eva became ready to gain deeper understanding with another active experience as she clapped her hands and mouthed the word "Become." Once again in the green haze, Eva jogged in the park with her best friend, Candice. Candice expressed her concern about her husband, Bob's depression. He appeared to be in a dark place, a dark night of his soul. He was a very conscientious man but due to several uncontrollable turns in fate, his business had suffered. Bob was having trouble sleeping, and had become distant and irritable.

Together Eva and Candice hatched a plan that would encourage Bob to dream again about what he did best, and bring back the joy and passion he'd once felt for his life-calling so he could fulfill his personal mission, whatever the cost. The plan worked. Bob's depression soon lifted and he was back working passionately at what he loved to do.

The night before the launch of his first planned project, they all ate a celebratory meal at a local restaurant. Everyone present toasted with prayers and blessings for the future. Returning to the car that evening, they found it covered with bird droppings.

"It's a sign." Eva squealed, knowing now that Bob's launch would be a phenomenal success. "Have faith, my friends, the bird droppings are a message, a blessing, an ancient folktale of good things to come! This synchronistic event supports my faith that everything is going to be just fine. There are signs and symbols in our outer world that reveal we are moving in the right direction. It's like a validation that the universe is agreeing with our plan."

The next week, the project came in – bringing with it financial rewards and security for years to come. Eva's intuition knew the signs from heaven had been interpreted with faith and delight. Bob was living his mission and the heavens had smiled.

Sophia and the Knight beamed. The Knight said, "There you have it, Eva. You have learned this with your whole being, organic learning we call it. If we had merely imparted the information to you, you wouldn't really know it with your whole being. But now that you've learned it experientially, you understand it with every cell of your being. It has become an integral part of you, and you will derive energy from it."

She continued, "Go ahead and test it, Eva. Close your eyes, meditate on someone you deeply love, allowing this love to expand your heart until you feel it burst with joy. Now open your eyes and look in the mirror."

Eva slowly opened her eyes and saw a massive green cloud of energy projected from her body, permeating the space around her. Big pink puffs bounced off the green cloud. "This is absolutely incredible."

The Knight raised a hand in caution. "Access to the higher spiritual domain of the sixth chamber is a deserving privilege reserved for only those persons who have done the work of the first, second, third, fourth, and fifth chambers. It is no easy task to enter the sixth chamber. With it comes enormous responsibility. You are now seeing with your third eye. The left eye, or the eye of the masculine, is that which you use when you negotiate in your everyday world. It reveals polarity, division, the separateness of things. It is a structural template for successful living on the earth. The right eye is of the feminine energy, intuition and knowing, the eye of nurturing and care-taking that the left eye does not posses the hardware for.

"The right eye is the inner eye and can see planes in the interior world that the left cannot. The third eye, the eye located in the center of the brain between the left and the right, is the bridge between the two, and is not normally seen in this physical world, but is known when one sees from it, as you have. Only when the left and the right eyes' vision is in a healthy balance that allows the third eye, the eye of Sophia energy, that perfect balance of masculine and feminine, to see. The third eye is wisdom, grace, connection, assimilation. The picture it views is that of wholeness, the largest and most profound truth in the universe. The separateness and limitation of the world viewed from the left eye alone, the eye of the masculine, or the right eye alone, the eye of the feminine, creates an illusion. The reality is that everything in the universe is joined by energy.

The Sixth Chamber

"The implications of this are vast and far-reaching. If everything is one, when we cause pain to another, it is akin to sliding a knife in your own gut. So if you hurt another, the pain comes back to you as a more forceful momentum and hits you at an even higher speed than it went out.

"Now allow me to introduce you to Artemis, goddess of the hunt and moon."

Artemis, dark-skinned and athletic, sprinted forward in her huntress attire, leather top and pants with a bow and arrow at her side. "The sixth chamber is a place of setting and reaching goals, of independence, autonomy, and ironically, deep connections, with your deepest sense of connection coming from within. You love others and feel loyalty, along with a deep connectivity to them. You are part of them and they are part of you, but you are not dependent on that for your sense of well-being. It is also the domain of the 'wild woman,' the part of our feminine energy that deeply connects to nature, wildlife, and to our deepest inner selves."

Artemis continued, "In your world, Eva, only a small percentage of the human mind-potential has been tapped, using the brain as operating equipment."

"Why?" Eva asked.

"Because your society places more value on rational, linear thinking skills, the brain's full capacity has not been utilized."

"How can we learn to use the part that seems to be lying dormant?" asked Eva.

"By tapping into the unconscious mind and learning to use it effectively. All matter, even subtle thought matter, consists of particles, or charges of electricity, negative (electrons) and positive (protons). These particles stay in a perpetual 'dance' with each other, continually interacting, causing vibrations, which form a certain wave pattern known as frequency."

Sophia added, "Yes, and thought becomes a powerful force for change and is greatly influenced by visualization – holding an image in the mind's eye."

Artemis continued, "The left, rational brain, is of time and space, the material world as we know it with our five senses. The right brain operates outside of time and space, in the realm of the eternal – the spiritual. Through the exercise of visualization, imagery, meditation, art, play, and creative activity, the dormant mind can be activated and utilized, for personal and universal enhancement and transformation. Each person can be empowered to change themselves, the world, and the universe by firm belief. Belief holds the vision form in the mind's eye to manifest into reality. The forces of sub-atomic physics are harnessed in the dancing electrons of thought matter, sending the visual out into the universal electrical field to draw the desired vision into physical form. It is as profound and simple as that."

Sophia said, "As is the law of love, the most powerful force in the universe and the most sought. To receive the love we desire, we must learn to give. The love we send out into the world will come back to us ten-fold of the form in which it was sent. This is what poets, painters, and writers have revealed to us in the form of metaphors through their art."

Artemis added, "Yes. With this ability and gift to see with the third eye comes an awesome responsibility on the part of the seer. As with all the other rooms, there is, in our humanity, a part of our being that is vulnerable to the seven deadly sins. In each room, as you have seen, there is one deadly sin of which you are vulnerable, because of the particular work required to enter the room.

"In the noble sixth chamber, the deadly sin is that of vainglory, or excessive pride of the ego, of taking the higher knowing and using it for the benefit of self-aggrandizement, to impress others, to inflate your lower self or the ego, to make yourself appear superior. Vainglorious activities do nothing but promote separateness, and the actions are based on the limited ego, which thrives on fear. You must take care to live in humility at all times. If you choose not to move forward, if you use your gifts for personal gratification or acquisition and not as a tool to edify yourself, others and the world, you will surely fall, and the fall from this height is much more dangerous and difficult to recover from.

"Treasure your gift, this fruit of the spirit – peace. Take it with you, child, and use it for the purposes of God, and you will be filled with a peace beyond all comprehension. Fear will never reside in you, for you know that there is nothing in this universe to fear. There is nothing on this earth that can harm your soul or your spirit, for that is the essence of you, the unique form of energy living, growing, and changing into God-given infinity."

The Seventh Chamber

Pure white/silver/gold chamber – crown energy center

"Instead, seek his kingdom, and these other things will be given you besides."

— *Luke 12:31* [14]

"Extol her, and she will exalt you; she will bring you honors if you embrace her;
She will put on your head a graceful diadem; a glorious crown will she bestow on you."

— *Proverbs 4:8-9* [15]

SOPHIA AND THE KNIGHT walked on either side of Eva as they approached the steps leading to the inner chamber of the castle, the highest of chambers, and the location of the seventh chamber. Sophia handed Eva a single red rose, along with a shimmering white lace and satin dress.

Sophia said, "Eva, this is your wedding dress. You have purified yourself and are now ready for complete union with the divine. You have learned much, worked hard to balance the masculine and feminine energies within and are prepared adequately for this momentous occasion. The most important thing for you to do now is not to think much, but to love much. Your energy system is clear and vibrant, uncontaminated by festering wounds and dead wood. In the seventh chamber your marriage with the divine spirit will happen. With this sacred union comes a joy that holds no bounds. Now let us prepare for the ceremony."

Eva, awestruck by the simplicity and beauty of Sophia's words, stepped up to the altar to prepare herself for the occasion. Eva's eyes filled with tears, a natural result of being in the divine presence. Sophia began weaving delicate white and purple flowers around a tiara of silver and gold, and placed it on the crown of Eva's head.

The Knight walked up. "This is your *helmet of salvation*, Eva, and here is your *band of gold*, the eternal circle representing the completeness of your soul. God is central to the castle, residing in the seventh chamber, the seventh energy center of the body. God is central to the human being and our relationship to this divine energy defines our soul. Divineness of the seventh room seeks to permeate out into all the lower chambers of the castle."

As they joined the Knight for the walk into the center of the seventh chamber, open to the heavens above, they heard a beautiful melody from a harp, joined by seven trumpets, along with a chorus of angel-like voices.

The Knight warned, "There will come a dazzling display of white light such as you have never seen. Do not hesitate to shield your eyes until they adjust to such purity. You are now approaching your re-union with the Creator. When you incarnated into your human body, separating temporarily and partially from the divine, you began to experience a yearning to reconnect with God for that ultimate sense of completion and immersion. Now you will have it, as much as you can experience it in this world, in this body, knowing that you still have work to do. It does not stop here; it commences here. You will take peace and joy back into the world and do your best work, the service you came into this world to do."

Sophia added, "You must be careful of the deadly sin of the seventh chamber, which is that of greed. This is the most pervasive of all the deadly sins and runs rampant in your world today. If you have done your work, Eva, you are not likely to be endangered by this pull. It happens to the ones who try to gain entry into the seventh chamber unlawfully, before they have done their inner work, who become prey for the deadly energy that will surely pounce. These people are not prepared spiritually for the room, they only wish to hoard and take, to fill up their empty vessel."

When they reached the high center platform of the inner chamber, the question for entry into the seventh room formed in Eva's mind. "What must I do to be whole – in body, mind, and spirit?"

A dazzling image of Aphrodite flew in from the top of the castle, landing softly on the floor of the inner chamber. Eva had never seen a more radiant woman. "*Kali speda*, Eva. I'm Aphrodite, goddess of love, and feminine herald of the seventh chamber. I'm here to answer your question on what you must do to be whole in body, mind, and spirit. I get criticized as a goddess for being pleasure-oriented, loving my sensuous nature, and being in the moment. This can make some people feel uncomfortable with me. Many people in your culture put negative connotations on this, thinking I'm lewd and lustful. The truth is, God gave us the gifts of deep pleasure and sensuous feelings, the eros, that which is the heaven within, the yearning for and union with God. The physical experience of spiritual union, merging the divine masculine and divine feminine, held in tension during those few moments of bliss, is the experience we all long for; experiencing the Grail for a moment in time. During those pinnacle moments of ultimate pleasure, one is allowed a glimmer of his face, and a taste of the bliss of eternal union.

"Eros has become distorted and limited to sexuality in the form of hedonistic eroticism. We must learn to use the eros energy, in conjunction with our spirituality, as something deep and sacred. You only have to ask if you're using that energy to honor your ego or your high self. If you use it to express love, and to enhance the energy of humankind, you will experience deep sensual beauty and enjoyment. It's as simple as that. If you use it for the enhancement of your lower self, or ego, you will fall into serial relationships, promiscuity, and impulsiveness, which will only lead to self-destruction."

"That is beautiful, Aphrodite. I love the Corinthian scripture about what love is. This helps me to understand the idea of love in regards to the sacred contract. Husband and wife cleave one to another until death do they part, honoring and adoring each other. Their intimacy is a gift to be treasured before God. Thank you for impressing upon me just how precious this love is."

Suddenly a brilliant light exploded into the room, nearly blinding Eva – a light tinged with purple, gold, and silver threads. Then a river of joy flooded over her, a joy she had never before experienced. She knew her work in the other rooms had prepared her for this magnificent place, this place she knew instinctively held her Holy Grail.

Sophia and the Knight stepped forward with Eva to light the unity candle. The chorus of angels lifted the celestial music to an octave so high that Eva thought she would burst with joy. She stepped forward to the altar, where an ornately carved, silver and gold chalice sat in the center.

Together Sophia and the Knight walked to the back of the altar and lifted the goblet to Eva's lips. The Knight spoke, "Eva, you have now found your Holy Grail, the perfect blend and balance of the highest nature of the masculine and feminine. Drink from the flask of the masculine, which is the structure and container, the vessel for the life-giving feminine spirit. Please partake of the wine, that of the earth, the Sophia energy, and let it flow through you and from you, and then back out into the world. We seek the Holy Grail and the Holy Grail seeks us – with this the sacred marriage occurs."

Eva's mind takes her to thoughts about how many times she drank wine from a chalice but never understood its symbolic significance. The fruits come from the earth, from Sophia energy. Now she realizes how all the fruits of the spirit purely come together at the time of communion with a reverence for the holy, in the holiest moment. The wine cannot be available to us without a form to hold it. Eva thinks out loud, "Communion is like looking out over a beautiful horizon, where the earth and sky meet. It's no wonder Jesus turned water into wine for so many." Eva's thoughts are interrupted with beautiful chanting.

Sophia and the Knight chanted together the Lord's Prayer in Aramaic, as they joined the holy spirit present in the Communion.

"We have now found our Holy Grail. We have infused the masculine structure with the wine, the stream of life energy of Sophia, the feminine face of god, creating a balance, which has healed our wounded mind, body, and spirit. We are now free. We are separate and we are one. We are male and we are female. We are dark and we are light. We are one with the spirit. We are the Holy Grail and the Holy Grail is us, in all our wholeness, in all our holiness."

The Knight said, "Come. It is time for the feast of celebration, the feast of the bride and bridegroom, the dinner of eternal life. Let us partake of the fruits with Persephone, Demeter, Hestia, Hera, Athena, Artemis, and Aphrodite."

Sophia added, "Go back into the world, Eva, and with more love than you know. Keep your castle clean and warm, visit the rooms often. Know that we are always with you, within you. And always remember how very much you are loved."

After kissing her on the cheek, the Knight and Sophia dissolved into tiny lights before her eyes. And then there was nothing. And there was everything – the holy spirit in all completion of the moment. Overwhelmed again with emotion, Eva's eyes filled with tears, and she was filled with the peace, joy, love, and completeness that Sophia and the Knight promised her.

Eva walked slowly, quietly, down each step, with a stillness in her heart like she had never experienced. As she passed through each chamber, she noticed how different everything appeared in the interior castle.

Eva knows it is time to exit the castle doors, time to go back to her world – in joyful service to her fellow man. Her task now is to put her faith into action.

As she walks out of the golden castle into the blinding sunlight, Eva looks

The Seventh Chamber

back and realizes that every event and experience in her life has been purposeful and presented an opportunity for growth. She can now live in a state of reverence, faithful to the call – leaving it all to the Creator. Each piece of the mosaic fits together in a beautiful pattern of her life's mission, designed by the feminine energy of Sophia. Every thread interwoven through her life has been necessary for the tapestry to be complete. She will only see the full picture when she enters heaven – a heaven so dazzling the colors would surely blind human eyes.

She can now fully trust and turn her existence over to the Christ within, knowing she is in good hands while she fulfills her tasks on earth. She will live the questions, live into the future, live the journey, live with peace, and live her empowerment. Eva remembers how Miriam supported Moses' journey. How blessed it will be to step her toe into the world each day and faithfully watch as the sea parts. Now Eva too knows she holds her own power, and that power emanates from the source of all goodness, the God within.

Eva's Reflection

EVA STRUGGLED to open her eyes, sunlight streaming through the window. Chris was looking down at her, gently shaking her shoulder. "Honey, are you okay? You have tears rolling down your face."

Eva smiled, gently brushing the tears away with the back of her hand. "I'm fine, Chris. These are tears of joy. I just had a *big* dream – and it felt so real."

Sitting up in bed, Eva took Chris' hand in hers. "Will you please just sit here with me while I tell you about it? I don't want to forget a single detail."

Chris gave her a quizzical look, and then wrapped her in his arms. "Sure, honey, I want to hear everything."

Slowly and deliberately Eva began relating the story to Chris. "I entered a castle, much like the ones I'd read about in Cinderella when I was young. When I read that story long ago, I never gave any thought to what happened after Cinderella married the Prince and went to live *beyond the castle doors.* I wish the writers had finished the story to teach all of us what to expect in this less-than-perfect life. I don't believe Cinderella 'lived happily ever after.' When the castle doors closed behind her, the honeymoon ended and her life challenges were just beginning! She had to confront demons in all shapes and sizes, and confront obstacles around every corner. Just as significant, she had to helplessly watch her loved ones experience painful life woes. But in my dream, which seemed to be the last half of the Cinderella story, I watched a modern day Cinderella grow into a woman of wisdom, from maiden to crone. Through this interior castle journey she was transformed and healed of her wounds. She watched dramas and experiences from a place of understanding, seeing with new eyes."

Chris's eyes held fascination as she shared her story and he tenderly held her hands in his. "Without going through the entire castle journey, through the seven chambers, I'd rather think out loud about what this dream is trying to tell me and what I'm supposed to learn."

Eva's Reflection

Eva continued, "Finding the Holy Grail doesn't change the reality: the fact that evil exists in the world. Yet there's a peace, a loving reassurance that life is as it should be, and more importantly, we're never alone. Now I feel Christ's love and Sophia's wisdom before me. I feel compelled to pass the 'good news' to all who will listen, starting with you. I understand the importance of this feminine aspect of myself that was undeveloped and undervalued in me and in the world around me. I understand the importance of listening to my heart as though I'm listening to the heart and mind of Jesus and Mary, perfect examples of Sophia wisdom. These ideas are not written laws that govern, but a way to natural discernment that is realized through prayer. This enables us to realize a personal relationship with God and understand the feminine side of God, the way of Sophia. In time I will explain what I've learned about her.

"Chris, I realize through this dream we all write our own stories and naturally live into them. There's so much inner healing that takes place just by telling your story. Someone told me years ago that you can bear anything if you can tell a story about it. I understand this now. You and I are living our own modern-day myth. The gift is this: we have an opportunity to write the rest of our story now. We can become hero and heroine or choose a tragic ending.

Chris's eyes glistened "Honey, you didn't have a dream – you went on a journey."

"Yes, I did – a life-changing one. Now I'm ready to go out and teach what I've learned. It's not going to be easy, and believe me, that peaceful castle is a tempting sanctuary. But I know God is with me – he's with us – and he'll carry us through anything we have to face. But right now I just feel like… dancing!"

Eva walked outside her home, the dew from the grass sparkling in the sun. She took a deep breath and looked up at the sky. Interesting, the moon was still in the sky as the sun found its place in the blue heavens. Then she began her dance – barefoot before the sun and the moon.

The Holy Grail

"Before all ages, in the beginning, he created me,
and through all ages I shall not cease to be."

— Sirach 24:9 xvi

WE HAVE NOW FOUND our Holy Grail. We have infused the masculine structure of God, the divine father, symbolized by the beautifully shaped, strong, and ornate silver chalice, with the stream of life energy of Sophia, the feminine face of God, creating a balance, which has healed our wounded mind, body, and spirit. We are now free. We are separate, and we are one. We are male, and we are female. We are dark and we are light. We are human, and we are divine. We are unique, and we are of God. We are the Holy Grail, and the Holy Grail is us – in all our wholeness, in all our holiness. Namaste.

"Peace I leave with you; my peace I give to you. Not as the
world gives do I give it to you. Do not let your hearts be
troubled or afraid."

— John 14:27 17

The Holy Grail

BENEFICENT FEMININE

To be known not as a word,
  To be understood not as a feeling,
    or merely an energy

SHE who was a beginning,
who imagined along with the powers of
great unnameable, unanswerable forces,
Propelled by the strength of Love unattainable,
only borrowed, carefully.

SHE
who knew of love without boundaries,
stretching across the generous miles
of Her bosom, rounded belly of Her growing womb,
A womb whose place lay first among the heavens,
and whose calling blanketed the earths rocks
and mountains.
Permeating the plants, trees,
Infusing
the Creators with encouragement
for a grand PLAN.

May Creation bow before for Her guiding hand,

Man and Wo(mb)-an,

SHE who gave,
Her portion of the vastness,
a devotion so tender,
a bestowing of rhythm,
a beating,
so loud in the ears of who may
be honored enough to hear,
Down through the ages,
Down into the crevasses, the folds of canyons.

BEYOND THE CASTLE DOORS

Blending with the rivers waters, merging into
the mouth of seas,
All symbols of Her flesh,
The pillars of the World temples echo Her bones.

SHE
who holds up Her end of the work,
Her agreement of the bargain,

Not to be known through words,
   Not be understood as a feeling

SHE
Whose radiance shall shine upon the Path
through the lights beyond measuring,
rising upward
in the stem of every being.

SHE
whose dialect of sensitivity flows through the veins
of all who walk over our Good Earth,
Proceed through the Gates of Her Reverence,
One is safe and sound within Her wondrous gift of
receptivity.

— *Billie M. Fair-Fontaine*

PART II

SECTION 1
Sophia References

SECTION 2
Historical Icons of Sophia Energy

SECTION 3
Archetypes of the Goddesses

SECTION 4
Symbols, Goddesses,

The Return of Sophia

"We will not listen to what you say in the name of the LORD.
Rather will we continue doing what we had proposed; we will
burn incense to the queen of heaven and pour out libations to
her, as we and our fathers, our kings and princes have done in the
cities of Judah and the streets of Jerusalem. Then we had enough
food to eat and we were well off; we suffered no misfortune.
But since we stopped burning incense to the queen of heaven and
pouring out libations to her, we are in need of everything and are
being destroyed by the sword and by hunger."

— *Jeremiah 44:16-18* [18]

SOPHIA, the feminine aspect of God, is an archetypal image of the earth, of
death, of healing, transcendence, and transformation. She has remained a vital
component of our psyche and collective unconscious, even though her energy
has been repressed and ignored throughout the ages. Sophia evokes life, death,
resurrection, restoration, and renewal. Her myriad faces and diverse character
are personified in mythology in the form of the goddesses. In Greek, the word
"Sophia" means "wisdom." So in The New American Bible, Saint Joseph Edition
references, you can replace the word "wisdom" with the word "Sophia." This
then gives you a very different perspective on the scriptures.

When Sophia's rites and images are oppressed, she manifests in other forms
– dream symbolism, life impulses, and the Black Madonna figure. She remains
a constant in nature's rhythms. When the goddess energy is sparked in a person, via viewing of a great film, literary work, or painting, she is reborn, and her
energy shifts the consciousness of the person – becoming a catalyst for change
by transforming them. They become seized with responsibility to activate the
gifts of their spirit and become heroes of their own journey.

The Return of Sophia

The goddess energy lives within every human being. In a culture that dismisses her energy in favor of an exclusively male deity, the society becomes a spiritual wasteland and its very existence becomes endangered. Without the balancing energy of Sophia, chaos, violence, greed, and corruption reign. Sophia desires empowerment, harmony, and sovereignty so the life force in every person is allowed full expression.

As you read the story, listen to the goddesses as they whisper divine secrets of the ages, and follow them through the seven chambers as they give you the grand tour of consciousness and the spirit.

Sophia Quotes

GLIMPSES OF SOPHIA are found everywhere, in paintings, song, dance, and the written text. The following quotes are some of the written acknowledgements of her existence.

"A great sign appeared in the sky, a woman clothed with the sun, with the moon under her feet, and on her head a crown of twelve stars."

— Revelation 12:1 [19]

"For Jews demand signs and Greeks look for wisdom, but we proclaim Christ crucified, a stumbling block to Jews and foolishness to Gentiles, but to those who are called, Jews and Greeks alike, Christ the power of God and the wisdom of God."

— 1 Corinthians 1:22-23 [20]

"For the foolishness of God is wiser than human wisdom, and the weakness of God is stronger than human strength."

— 1 Corinthians 1:25 [21]

"It is due to him that you are in Christ Jesus, who became for us wisdom from God, as well as righteousness, sanctification, and redemption,"

— 1 Corinthians 1:30 [22]

Sophia Quotes

"Yet we do speak a wisdom to those who are mature, but
not a wisdom of this age, nor of the rulers of this age who
are passing away.

Rather, we speak God's wisdom, mysterious, hidden,
which God predetermined before the ages for our glory,
and which none of the rulers of this age knew; for if they
had known it, they would not have crucified the Lord of
glory."

— *1 Corinthians 2:6-8* [23]

In the above quotes Paul is forthright in his claim that Jesus is our *Sophia*. One
of *Sophia's* traits Paul reveals is her hidden presence in all things – they come
into being only with her participation. He invests Jesus *Sophia* with restoring
hope of restoration of all things and persons.

"Rather, we speak God's wisdom, mysterious, hidden,
which God predetermined before the ages for our glory,"

— *1 Corinthians 2:7* [24]

"Now to him who can strengthen you, according to my
gospel and the proclamation of Jesus Christ, according to
the revelation of the mystery kept secret for long ages"

— *Romans 16:25* [25]

"and to bring to light [for all] what is the plan of the mystery
hidden from ages past in God who created all things,
so that the manifold wisdom of God might now be made
known through the church to the principalities and
authorities in the heavens.
This was according to the eternal purpose that he accom-
plished in Christ Jesus our Lord,
in whom we have boldness of speech and confidence of access
through faith in him."

— *Ephesians 3:9-12* [26]

"The first man never finished comprehending wisdom,
nor will the last succeed in fathoming her.
For deeper than the sea are her thoughts; her counsels,
than the great abyss."

— Sirach 24:26-27[27]

"Wisdom sings her own praises, before her own people
she proclaims her glory;
In the assembly of the Most High she opens her mouth,
in the presence of his hosts she declares her worth:
'From the mouth of the Most High I came forth,
and mistlike covered the earth. In the highest heavens
did I dwell, my throne on a pillar of cloud.
The vault of heaven I compassed alone,
through the deep abyss I wandered."

— Sirach 24:1-5[28]

"There is but one, wise and truly awe-inspiring, seated
upon his throne:
It is the Lord; he created her, has seen her and taken
note of her.
He has poured her forth upon all his works,
upon every living thing according to his bounty;
he has lavished her upon his friends."

— Sirach 1:6-8[29]

"Or who ever knew you counsel, except you had given
Wisdom and sent your holy spirit from on high?"

— Wisdom 9:17[30]

"For discipline is like her name, she is not accessible to many.
Listen, my son, and heed my advice; refuse not my counsel.
Put your feet into her fetters, and your neck under her yoke."

— Sirach 6:23-25[31]

Sophia Quotes

Hebrew scriptures contain more about *Sophia* than almost any other figure in The New American Bible, Saint Joseph Edition. Yet she has been deliberately and strategically ignored. She clearly posed a threat to the authoritarian rule of the day. *Sophia*, being proud, assertive, angry, threatening, creative and energetic, threatened the patriarchal church stronghold, so they repressed and ignored her. Independence was discouraged in women so they buried any model of it. *Sophia* dominates the first nine chapters of Proverbs, yet most Protestant focus is on the later chapters.

Who is **Sophia**? She is **Wisdom,** she is **Discipline.**

> "For she is an aura of the might of God and a pure effusion of the glory of the Almighty; therefore nought that is sullied enters into her."
>
> — Wisdom 7:25 [32]

> "And she, who is one, can do all things, and renews everything while herself perduring; And passing into holy souls from age to age, she produces friends of God and prophets."
>
> — Wisdom 7:27 [33]

> "When he established the heavens I was there, when he marked out the vault over the face of the deep; When he made firm the skies above, when he fixed fast the foundations of the earth; When he set for the sea its limit, so that the waters should not transgress his command; Then was I beside him as his craftsman, and I was his delight day by day, Playing before him all the while, playing on the surface of his earth; and I found delight in the sons of men."
>
> — *Proverbs 8:27-31* [34]

> "Beyond health and comeliness I loved her, And I chose to have her rather than the light, because the splendor of her never yields to sleep. Yet all good things together came to me in her company, and countless riches at her hands."
>
> — *Wisdom 7:10-11* [35]

"Fullness of wisdom is fear of the LORD;
she inebriates men with her fruits."

— *Sirach 1:14* [36]

"Before all things else wisdom was created;
and prudent understanding, from eternity."

— *Sirach 1:4* [37]

"The LORD begot me, the first-born of his ways,
the forerunner of his prodigies of long ago;"

— *Proverbs 8:22* [38]

"Who has gone up to the heavens and taken her,
or brought her down from the clouds?
Who has crossed the sea and found her,
bearing her away rather than choice gold?
None knows the way to her,
nor has any understood her paths.
Yet he who knows all things knows her;
he has probed her by his knowledge –
He who established the earth for all time, and filled it with
four-footed beasts;"

— *Baruch 3:29-32* [39]

"Hear, O children, a father's instruction,
be attentive, that you may gain understanding!
Yes, excellent advice I give you;
my teaching do not forsake.
When I was my father's child, frail,
yet the darling of my mother,
He taught me, and said to me:
'Let your heart hold fast my words:
keep my commands, that you may live!
'Get wisdom, get understanding!

Sophia Quotes

Do not forget or turn aside from the words I utter.
Forsake her not, and she will preserve you;
love her, and she will safeguard you;"

— *Proverbs 4:1-6* [40]

"Hold fast to instruction, never let her go;
keep her, for she is your life."

— *Proverbs 4:13* [41]

"The beginning of wisdom is: get wisdom;
at the cost of all you have, get understanding.
Extol her, and she will exalt you;
she will bring you honors if you embrace her;
She will put on your head a graceful diadem;
a glorious crown will she bestow on you."

— *Proverbs 4:7-9* [42]

"For Wisdom is mobile beyond all motion,
and she penetrates and pervades all things
by reason of her purity."

— *Wisdom 7:24* [43]

"Resplendent and unfading is Wisdom,
and she is readily perceived by those
who love her, and found by those who seek her.
She hastens to make herself known
in anticipation of her men's desire;
he who watches for her at dawn
shall not be disappointed,
for he shall find her sitting by his gate.
For taking thought of her is the perfection
of prudence, and he who for her sake keeps
vigil shall quickly be free from care;

Because she makes her own rounds,
seeking those worthy of her,
and graciously appears to them in the ways,
and meets them with all solicitude."

— Wisdom 6:12-16 [44]

"Wisdom cries aloud in the street,
in the open squares she raises her voice;
Down the crowded ways she calls out,
at the city gates she utters her words:
'How long, you simple ones, will you love inanity,
how long will you turn away at my reproof?
Lo! I will pour out to you my spirit,
I will acquaint you with my words."

— Proverbs 1:20-23 [45]

"Does not Wisdom call, and Understanding raise
her voice? On the top of the heights along the road,
at the crossroads she takes her stand;
By the gates at the approaches of the city,
in the entryways she cries aloud:
'To you, O men, I call; my appeal is to the children
of men. You simple ones, gain resource, you fools,
gain sense. 'Give heed! For noble things I speak;
honesty opens my lips. Yes, the truth my mouth
recounts, but the wickedness my lips abhor.
Sincere are all the words of my mouth, no one of
them is wily or crooked; All of them are plain to
the man of intelligence, and right to those who attain
knowledge. Receive my instruction in preference to
silver, and knowledge rather than choice gold.
(For Wisdom is better than corals, and no choice
possessions can compare with her.)"

— Proverbs 8:1-11 [46]

Sophia Quotes

"Send her forth from your holy heavens and from your glorious throne dispatch her That she may be with me and work with me, that I may know what is your pleasure."

— *Wisdom 9:10* [47]

"For the deliberations of mortals are timid, and unsure are our plans. For the corruptible body burdens the soul and the earth shelter weighs down the mind that has many concerns."

— *Wisdom 9:14-15* [48]

"With me are riches and honor, enduring wealth and prosperity."

— *Proverbs 8:18* [49]

"Knowledge and full understanding she showers down; she heightens the glory of those who possess her."

— *Sirach 1:17* [50]

"Get wisdom, get understanding!
Do not forget or turn aside from the words I utter.
Forsake her not, and she will preserve you;
love her, and she will safeguard you;
The beginning of wisdom is: get wisdom;
at the cost of all you have, get understanding.
Extol her, and she will exalt you;
she will bring you honors if you embrace her;"

— *Proverbs 4:5-8* [51]

"She adds to nobility the splendor of companionship with God; even the LORD of all loved her."

— *Wisdom 8:3* [52]

"And if riches be a desirable possession in life,
what is more rich than Wisdom,
who produces all things?"

— *Wisdom 8:5* [53]

"Stoop your shoulders and carry her
and be not irked at her bonds.
With all your soul draw close to her;
with all your strength keep her ways.
Search her out, discover her;
seek her and you will find her.
Then when you have her,
do not let her go."

— *Sirach 6:26-28* [54]

"So I determined to take her to live with me,
knowing that she would be my counselor while all was
well, and my comfort in care and grief."

— *Wisdom 8:9* [55]

"Within my dwelling, I should take my repose beside her;
For association with her involves no bitterness and living
with her no grief, but rather joy and gladness."

— *Wisdom 8:16* [56]

"Her I loved and sought after from my youth;
I sought to take her for my bride and was enamored
of her beauty.
She adds to nobility the splendor of companionship
with God; even the LORD of all loved her."

— *Wisdom 8:2-3* [57]

Sophia Quotes

"Wisdom instructs her children and
admonishes those who seek her.
He who loves her loves life;
those who seek her out win her favor.
He who holds her fast inherits glory;
wherever he dwells, the Lord bestows blessings.
Those who serve her serve the Holy One;
those who love her the Lord loves.
He who obeys her judges nations;
he who hearkens to her dwells in her inmost chambers.
If one trusts her, he will possess her;
his descendants too will inherit her.
She walks with him as a stranger,
and at first she puts him to the test;
Fear and dread she brings upon him
and tries him with her discipline;
With her precepts she puts him to the proof,
until his heart is fully with her.
Then she comes back to bring him
happiness and reveal her secrets to him."

— *Sirach 4:11-18* [58]

"She is the book of the precepts of God,
the law that endures forever;
All who cling to her will live,
but those will die who forsake her.
Turn, O Jacob, and receive her:
walk by her light toward splendor."

— *Baruch 4:1-2* [59]

Sophia is co-creator with God, queen of heaven, a messenger of God, lover of God.

> "Whence, then, comes wisdom,
> and where is the place of understanding?
> It is hid from the eyes of any beast;
> from the birds of the air it is concealed.
> Abbaddon and Death say,
> 'Only by rumor have we heard of it.'
> God knows the way to it;
> it is he who is familiar with its place."

— *Job 28:20-23* [60]

> "For she is an aura of the might of God
> and a pure effusion of the glory of the Almighty;
> therefore nought that is sullied enters into her.
> For she is the refulgence of eternal light,
> the spotless mirror of the power of God,
> the image of his goodness."

— *Wisdom 7:25-26* [61]

The Two Marys Bible

DURING THE COURSE of history, the two Marys prominent in Jesus' life have weathered many a theological and political storm. Recently, historical and Christian church scholars have uncovered new evidence regarding the prominence of both Marys in Jesus' life. Traditionally, St. Mary, mother of Jesus, has acquired the reverence of a Madonna, whereas Mary Magdalene has been portrayed as the prostitute, even though scholarship and New Testament transcripts reveal she was Jesus' lead apostle and his beloved. Ironically, these are the two archetypal roles western civilization has used to view the woman's role in society, sometimes known as "whore-madonna complex."

Due to in-depth scholarly studies, Mary Magdalene's rightful position as primary disciple is in the process of being restored and St. Mary has become humanized, making it easier for people to connect with her. Pope John Paul II so loved St. Mary he wore her image on his robes and head-wear. He professed openly of his belief that she interceded on his behalf and saved his life during his attempted assassination, and did so in order for him to complete his mission here on earth. The Pope struggled at times with maintaining a balance between his deep devotion and love for Mary and his love for her son, Jesus, feeling he was short-changing Jesus in his reverence for Mary.

St. Mary has been known by many names – Queen of Heaven, Bride of Christ, Mother of Mercy, and Mother of God. St. Mary was the first disciple, the first believer in Jesus as Son of God. She accepted the invitation, with total surrender, to bear God's son. Then she followed and supported Jesus during all his days on earth. When most others fled the crucifixion, she lay at the foot of the cross. St. Mary represents the mother, daughter, and holy soul of the world, the feminine icon of all history, the Sophia energy. She has appeared to more people throughout history than any other saint, and with her sightings she leaves hope for the world.

Mary Magdalene has only recently been given renewed respect as one of Jesus' lead disciples and his beloved. We do not have to answer the question about her relationship to Jesus to understand her prominent role in his life. The symbolic meaning behind her very name is revealing: *magdala* is a Hebrew word meaning "fort, watchtower, or stronghold." Evidence from the scriptures indicates she was his favorite and of prime importance in delivering his message to humanity. Jesus loved her as he loved all life, as he loved his people – children, women, the infirm, the poor, and all animals. He cast out seven demons from Mary and made her pure. This act was symbolic for his washing away the same seven deadly sins of all men, by virtue of his death on the cross. Mary proceeded to follow him for the rest of his life and dedicated the rest of her life to spreading his message.

Mary Magdalene was the first person Jesus appeared to when he was resurrected. Soon after, sightings of Mary were reported in France, where she was accompanied by a child. She reportedly died in a small French community surrounded by the protection of the Holy Spirit. Today Catholics and followers of other religious traditions pray to St. Mary as an intercessory to God the Father, Jesus the Son, and the Holy Spirit. Because of her feminine characteristics, the "giver of life" is receptive, nurturing, compassionate, understanding, gentle, and loving. St. Mary represents an icon of the divine feminine, the Sophia energy. She accepted the call to bear the greatest of gifts to the world – and she listens to all of our calls everyday.

Hildegard of Bingen

HILDEGARD was from the town of Bingen in Germany. She is remembered as a great poet, musician, painter, and a mystic who loved to study and write about nature, medieval medicine, and her visions of God. Hildegard followed a Benedictine way of life and became abbess of her convent. One of her major works called *Scivian* or *Know The Ways* has been called an encyclopedia of salvation. In it she writes about the search for "our original wisdom" and how we must recover this "elusive treasure." She also is recognized for her holistic healing practices, which are reflected in the way she lived her life. She thought it was important to enjoy life to its fullest, at the same time revere every sacred moment, and all of God's creation.

Hildegard is very inclusive. Her writings are based on her visions, in which God is expressed in female form. One of her visions is that of a woman searching for a lost silver coin, instead of a male shepherd searching for his lost sheep. She described God in feminine terms, as Mother. Her illuminations portray the Church (Ecclesia) with feminine characteristics. In Hildegard's time, the feminine images, which characterized the Church, were authenticated by Pope Eugene III. Without the Pope's stamp of validation, Hildegard's theology would have been confined to the twenty women in her monastery. The feminine attributes of God, Sophia energy, are carried through the Christian tradition by primarily Eastern Fathers of the Church and other women writers before and after Hildegard. However, Hildegard was the first woman theologian to write extensively.

At the time of her death it was reported that two streams of light formed a cross in the sky. Hildegard had always talked about how her visions came from the "living light" therefore how appropriate for the light to validate her teachings for us all.

Perpetua

Woman and Martyr born in AD 181

IMPRISONED AFTER GIVING BIRTH at the age of 22, Perpetua had a vision of a man milking sheep, who offered her milk in the form of curds...

A tall man dressed in a white robe at the top of the ladder was milking sheep. About him were many thousands dressed in white robes. The man in the shepherd's role raised his head, looked upon her and said, "Welcome child." He gave Perpetua some curds of the milk. Perpetua received it in the joined hands and ate it. Those in the white robes said, "Amen." Through her acceptance, Perpetua becomes a part of the heavenly community at the top of the ladder. The community receives her much as in a kind of initiation rite, with their acclamation "Amen."

The vision represents the quality of nurturing (Sophia energy) in relation to a Christ-like figure. In the vision, Perpetua embodies Sophia energy, found in the book of Revelation 12:1-3[62] "A great sign appeared in the sky, a woman clothed with the sun, with the moon under her feet, and on her head a crown of twelve stars. She was with child and wailed aloud in pain as she labored to give birth. Then another sign appeared in the sky; it was a huge red dragon, with seven heads and ten horns, and on its heads were seven diadems.[lxii]

In Perpetua's dream, like the woman in Revelation, she encounters a huge dragon, possibly representing evil energy or ignorance. Perpetua meets the dragon at the foot of the tall, golden ladder (the first room of the castle?) as she is about to ascend. Her dream account reports that she stepped on the head of the dragon (recognizing evil energy and ignorance for what it was) and proceeds to climb the ladder, dodging lances, hooks, and daggers on her ascent. This image of the woman conqueror, with the snake at her feet, is also associated with the Blessed Virgin in her liturgical hours, in the Eucharist prayers of certain feasts. Both the Blessed Virgin and Perpetua embody wisdom.

Perpetua was martyred in the amphitheater at Carthage at the command of the Emperor Serverus, AD 203.

Our Lady of Guadalupe

ON DECEMBER 9, 1531, Juan Diego hiked six miles, in freezing weather, through the mountains of Mexico to attend mass. Seemingly out of nowhere, his ears were filled with enchanting music and celestial singing. Juan squinted up to where the music came from and saw a cloud glowing in brilliant whiteness, a rainbow forming from its rays. Then he heard the voice of a young woman who appeared before him, the loveliest woman he had ever seen, imploring him to build a church in her honor on the hill, wherein she could receive and compassionately nurture all her suffering children. She instructed Juan to take the information to the bishop, with the promise of a sign that a bouquet of flowers would spring from the hilltop's frozen soil. To prove definitively that she was, in fact, the Mother of God, she left imprinted on Juan's coat a full-length color portrait of herself standing on the moon, the image seen to this very day in the cathedral of Mexico City.

Sophia in the Form of Miriam — Jewish Mother

ORTHODOX JEWISH TRADITION worships the family of Abraham, with few women included in the family tree. Jewish women are astutely aware of the imbalance and dis-ease created by this blatant omission (the Grail is an empty and lifeless structure without the life force of the feminine) and have countered this by creating groups of women gathered. They speak at the Passover Dinner, the Seder Dinner Christ would have had.

Hidden and ignored, Jewish women have virtually been eliminated from history. At the Seder Dinners, important Jewish women are remembered and honored. The Seder Dinner is to be experienced with the most special people in their lives. Hebrew language, family, and faith holds a long tradition and is the foundation of Christianity.

Jewish women have been relegated to a lowly position by the mandates of a patriarchal system, which is very much out of balance. For this reason, they are restoring their rightful place by enacting the Miriam's Cup ritual, created especially for the family Seder Dinner. Filling Miriam's cup follows the traditional second cup of wine, before the washing of hands. The women raise the empty goblet and say, "Miriam's cup is filled with water, rather than wine. I invite women of all generations at our Seder table to fill Miriam's cup with water from their own glasses." Miriam's cup is passed around the table as Miriam is remembered as a prophetess.

The significance of the ritual of filling Miriam's cup is illustrated by the following story. An ancient legend teaches that a miraculous well accompanied the Hebrews throughout their journey in the desert, providing them with water.

We fill Miriam's cup with water to honor her role in ensuring the survival of the Jewish people. Like Miriam, Jewish women in all generations have been essential for the continuity of our people. As keepers of traditions in the home, women passed down songs and stories, rituals, and recipes, from mother to daughter, from generation to generation. Let us drink from our glasses to draw from the strength and wisdom of our heritage.

When Miriam's cup is filled, the goblet is raised and the following words are recited, "We place Miriam's cup on our Seder table to honor the important role of Jewish women in our tradition and history, women whose stories have been too sparingly told. You abound in blessings, God, creator of the universe, who sustains us with living water. May we, like the children of Israel leaving Egypt, be guarded and nurtured and kept alive in the wilderness, and may you give us wisdom to understand that the journey itself holds the promise of redemption. Amen."

Stories are told of Jewish women who are admired, with the following dedication:

"Each Passover, we dedicate Miriam's Cup to a Jewish woman who has made important contributions in achieving equality and freedom for others. This year we honor…"

Dancing in honor of the prophetess, Miriam, follows the rituals for the prophet, Elijah, after the meal. Miriam's cup is lifted and the following is repeated:

"Miriam's life is a contrast to the life of Elijah, and both teach us important lessons. Elijah was a hermit who spent a large part of his time alone in the desert. He was a visionary and prophet, often very critical of the Jewish people, and focused on the messianic era. On the other hand, Miriam lived among her people in the desert following the path of *hesed*, or loving kindness. She constantly comforted the Israelites throughout their long journey, encouraging them when they lost faith. Therefore, Elijah's cup is a symbol of future messianic redemption, while Miriam's cup is a symbol of hope and renewal in the present. Thus, we need both Elijah's cup and Miriam's cup at our Seder table."

Next is much song and dance with tambourines. A tambourine is held up with a reading from *Exodus 15:20-21*:

"The prophetess Miriam, Aaron's sister, took a tambourine in her hand, while all the women went out after her with tambourines, dancing; and she led them in the refrain: Sing to the LORD, for he is gloriously triumphant; horse and chariot he has cast into the sea." [63]

The reader continues, "As Miriam once led the women of Israel in song and dance to praise God for the miracle of splitting the Red Sea, so we now rejoice and celebrate the freedom of the Jewish people today."

The Seder Dinner developed by Jewish women can be translated into a "Seder" celebration to honor any woman or women, in essence, honoring the Sophia energy, the reflection of the feminine face of God.

The Black Madonna

"He said in reply, 'I tell you, if they keep silent,
the stones will cry out!'"

— *Luke 19:40* [64]

THE BLACK MADONNA, portrayed since Neolithic times in the form of
paintings and statues of a dark maiden figure holding a dark child in her arms,
is a representation of the feminine face of God – Sophia. There are approxi-
mately 500 images of the Black Madonna in countries as far from each other as
France and Costa Rica. The chord the figure strikes within is one of archetypal
knowing, that of the earth, fertility, creativity, intuition, nurturing, enduring
love, and wisdom. The Black Madonna is the icon of the feminine, not in com-
petition for the altar of the masculine energy of God, but as its counterpart, its
balance, its equal, no more and no less.

The darkness represents the earth, the yin, the feminine, the night, the polar
aspect of the world and the universe from the light. For the collective unconscious, the darkness represents a willingness to embrace the darkness of the
soul, the night, a containment of the wisdom of Sophia that modern religion
has chosen to ignore or disdain through the centuries.

The Black Madonna archetype has recently begun to appear in the dreams
of thousands of American women and men. Many Jungian thinkers believe this
signifies the emergence of the long-latent, repressed feminine energy that has
been diminished in the predominantly patriarchal society. The energy is emerging because it is needed to keep the world from caving in on itself. Imbalance,
the scales weighing heavily on the side of male energy, will cause any system to
eventually self-destruct. The results of the emergence will be a new nurturing
and compassionate relationship with the planet and every living thing that
inhabits it.

The Black Madonna

If the Black Madonna archetype is not allowed to fully merge and manifest consciously, if it keeps getting pushed back under all the psychic layers, then it will spring out in dreams, images, and art forms. If continually ignored, it will eventually shut the body down until the archetype is attended to and allowed to energize the being.

The resurgence of interest in the Black Madonna has occurred at a time of history when her energy is most needed. The Black Madonna is a warm, loving, protective, and healing figure, embodied in this century by the ubiquitous Oprah Winfrey. People are instinctively drawn to her energy for support, wisdom, and healing. Her show has been at the top of the charts for a decade, her choices for book clubs have made the books automatic best sellers, her magazine is the top-selling one in America – and it is Oprah, our Black Madonna, who is always on the cover! We devour her words, her energy, and her spirit, but we also want to look at her! What does that say to us? That Oprah is the personification of the Sophia energy that has been buried for far too long and is now emerging to balance individuals, the nation, and the world of masculine energy. She is the archetype of deep healing – she represents the return and emergence of the divine Sophia energy.

Black is the color of the earth, representing fertility, creativity, and love. Ironically, the color black is not really a color, it absorbs all colors, is all-inclusive. The color black *is* all colors. The color black represents dark virgins in their majesty and organic power – the power in their strength, and in their enduring love. Black Madonna icons can be traced back to Neolithic times, a figure whose darkness embodied great creative powers, symbolizing fertility, intuitive powers, and great wisdom, an organic power springing from the earth and its connection with the life source of the heavens. Her grandest message is that darkness is good, it is from the darkness that the light springs free.

Darkness constitutes half of the twenty-four-hour day cycle. Darkness accounts for half of the universe. To live as a complete human being, part of the earth and part of the heavens is to dive down into the dark, murky depths of the soul and retrieve the treasure, bringing it back to the light and examining it and understanding it, polishing it up, then giving it as your gift to the world.

If we avoid the darkness because of fear, we miss the essence. Our lives become incomplete, lacking fulfillment. We feel restless, a dissatisfaction deep within that nothing or no one can fill. Our lives are lived on the surface, ever running from the restlessness through excessive busyness, distraction, or the acquisition of material things. To go into the darkness is a step toward living deeply, richly, and honoring our souls. To embrace the darkness is to embrace our soulfulness.

To see things clearly we must allow our eyes to adjust to the darkness. The light only blinds us at times. What does the darkness teach us? We learn about being still.

We learn about meditation and prayer, where deep healing and transformation take place. The Black Madonna is about embracing and trusting the darkness.

The light, representing the masculine energy of God, reveals separateness, illuminates things as they appear in the world of our five senses, necessary components for us to travel through our lives. But if this light is not balanced with the energies of the Black Madonna, the danger of becoming envious, pathologically competitive, striving for false power attained by acquisition of land and material status symbols, even other people is great. The terrified ego dominates, enclosed in its own self-centered universe. It is driven by fear of what happens to it if it breaks out of its comfortable container, so it defends its fortress with vengeance. However, if one perseveres, recognizing this, then the understanding will come, the knowing that a world of spirit lies beyond the limited structure of the ego, and that stepping into the spirit land is the only way to balance the ego with the life force.

When one takes the initiative to move into the spirit, the ego is forced to stay in its place, necessary but not the ruling force. Out of necessity, it will eventually adjust and do its job. If we choose not to move into the spirit and operate solely within the structure of the ego, we will become sick, individually, and universally: sick in the mind, body, and spirit. Without the necessary balance of the Sophia energy, the individual and the world runs amuck.

The resurgence of interest in the Black Madonna, directly and indirectly, reflected in Oprah's popularity, optimistically represents a return to the soul, a return to balance, offering us help and hope for individual and planetary healing. Oprah represents the wise, compassionate, and great mother whose arms are wide enough to embrace everyone and whose heart is large enough to send out her waves of loving feminine energy to all who will accept it. As an image of the divine Sophia, she is larger than life, available to everyone daily via the miracle of technology. The magazine, *Science and the Mind*, recently voted Oprah as "Spiritual Hero of the Year."

The Black Madonna

We must answer the call to embrace the feminine side of God, the Sophia energy, the blood and the water, the pure stream of life energy and pulsating life force, within the structure of the masculine container.

With an exclusive focus on the masculine face of God, through predominantly patriarchal conditioning, a restless current of energy continues to course through our veins. Many feel it as a sense of agitation, an innate dissatisfaction in life, no matter what has been attained and acquired. Deep within, where the still Sophia waters run deep, sits the Black Madonna, waiting to heal when we arrive. Then we find who we really are.

In the book of *Song of Songs 1:5-6*[65], the Bride takes voice:

"I am as dark – but lovely,
O daughters of Jerusalem –
As the tents of Kedar,
as the curtains of Salma.

Do not stare at me because I am swarthy,
because the sun has burned me.
My brothers have been angry with me;
they charged me with the care of the vineyards;
my own vineyard I have not cared for."

Whether we find Sophia in the Bride of the Song of Solomon, the Black Madonna, Cinderella, or through Eva in *Beyond the Castle Doors*, we recognize our need to know her. We want her to live in our hearts.

Sophia and Jesus Christ

"Or who ever knew your counsel, except you had given
wisdom and sent your holy spirit from on high?
And this were the paths of those on earth made straight,
and men learned what was your pleasure, and were saved
by Wisdom."

— *Wisdom 9:17-18*[66]

JESUS CHRIST PERSONIFIES the embodiment of the perfect balance of the masculine and feminine energies. The historical Jesus came into the world with his perfectly balanced energy to balance a world that had become imbalanced through a dominating patriarchal system. Jesus honored and loved animals, children, and women, thereby revering divine Sophia, evidenced in his deep love of Mary Magdalene, his primary apostle and human counterpart of the divine feminine.

Jesus came to reveal this perfect balance of masculine and feminine energies, revealed in his words, teachings, and actions. He showed that all limitations have human origins. In his actions, he demonstrated the full empowerment of the Christ energy – the perfectly balanced sacred masculine and sacred feminine, energies that exist in every man and every woman. By application of his example, are we all capable of miraculous works?

Simplicity was an essential quality of Christ's teachings while on this earth. He taught that to receive, we must give. When we cling or try to "hoard" energies, we block their flow. We find ourselves bogged down, weighted, and depressed with this stored energy. We cannot function optimally. Only when energy is allowed to flow freely through giving and receiving, being open, will we feel its power to manifest not only in our own lives, but that of others and the world.

Sophia and Jesus Christ

The key is to surrender to the high power, letting go of worry, fear, and possessiveness. Such surrender, in turn, opens our portal to divine essence. We must be willing to allow love to flow freely through our being. With this ultimate surrender, man or woman in this rightful arena will know no boundaries of space and time. We all have within us latent, God-given abilities, we simply have to open to receive them. Seek and know. Pray and meditate. Receive and send back blessings to the world.

With the advent of patriarchal societies, Sophia was deliberately misplaced, repressed, and oppressed. The misplaced energy of the matriarch manifests itself in the culture in massive, overwhelming need to control everything and everyone. This ubiquitous need is based on pure, unadulterated *fear*. The terrible events of the world are designed to tap into fears, to give certain individuals and institutions a false sense of power. Energy is depleted through the emotion of fear – as it causes chronic worry and anxiety. Our task is to refuse to give our energy to terrible events, viewing our own body as a temple where we don't allow entry of the negative. Then the world is infused and affected by our pure, positive energy radiating outward to counter the negative. We can learn to live in our center of calm and peace rather than entering into the chaotic turmoil of the world. Jesus remained unaffected by the negative as he carried his cross.

To remain in our inner sanctuary and experience personal growth, we must operate out of the balance of the masculine and feminine, the strong container and the wise, intuitive space, allowing these energies to merge within us without letting one dominate the other. Failure to open to the feminine within us is usually the result of fear of the ego, fear of being receptive to the unknown.

When we have the courage to move into the unknown, into the dark space where Sophia resides, we are operating in love and faith, releasing the limited ego's hold on the consciousness in order to access the feminine intuitive spirit. Then we feel that sense of oneness, the connection to all life that creates in us a fullness, a sense of abundant joy.

In our society, the desires of the ego have been catered to, fed, and are the source of addiction. Consequently, the natural movement of the Sophia energy through us, our opening of the floodgates to allow for Sophia energy to flow unobstructed, has been severely stunted.

To activate the Sophia, one must be aware. In this consciousness, one seeks and knows that the energy is there. Prayer and meditation, a quieting of the mind follows, then the act of listening and receiving.

Archetypes of the Goddesses

The Goddesses

Listen to the great gods and goddesses as they whisper divine secrets of the ages through symbols, metaphors, and archetypes. Follow them through the seven chambers as they give you the grand tour of consciousness and the spirit.

PERSEPHONE: Goddess of the underworld and death/first chamber/sacral area – She goes from innocence to consciousness, individuation, wisdom, and transformation.

DEMETER: Goddess of agriculture/second chamber/abdominal area – She is earth mother, in charge of creation, reproduction, and renewal of life.

HECATE: Goddess of the dark side of the moon/between second and third chamber: – She negotiates conscious and unconscious.

HESTIA: Goddess of the hearth and home/third chamber/solar plexus – She guards the eternal flame at center of the soul, holds the center.

HERA: Goddess of marriage/fourth chamber/heart center – She guards the male-female balance within.

ATHENA: Goddess of wisdom and craft/fifth chamber/throat area – She guards the intellectual and feminine independence.

ARTEMIS: Goddess of the moon and hunt/sixth chamber/third eye forehead – She guards individuality, independence, and laser-focus on goals.

APHRODITE: Goddess of beauty and love and goddess of compassion/seventh chamber/crown of the head –She exudes and revels in beauty, sensuality, warmth, and compassion.

Persephone

CHAMBER: First/red
Goddess of the underworld and death
Goddess of the first chamber/sacral
SYMBOLS: Seed, torch
DESCRIPTION: Little-girl-like

In Greek mythology, **PERSEPHONE** was the only daughter of Demeter and Zeus. Persephone was a carefree innocent who loved nature, particularly beautiful flowers, and playing with her young friends. While gathering flowers in a field one day, Hades suddenly appeared and abducted a terrified Persephone to his home in the underworld. Demeter was distraught and withdrew her energy from the world, and the earth became a barren wasteland. She finally forced Zeus to find a way to retrieve Persephone. Zeus promptly commissioned Hermes, the messenger god, to fetch Persephone.

When Hermes arrived in the underworld, he found a heavy-hearted Persephone, homesick for her mother and friends. She was overjoyed when Hermes told her he'd come to take her home. Before Hades would let her leave, he asked that she eat a pomegranate seed. When Persephone reunited with Demeter, Persephone told her about eating the pomegranate seed. Demeter told Persephone that eating the seed required her to spend one-third of the year in Hades, and two-thirds in the upper world with Demeter.

Eventually, Persephone was proclaimed queen of the underworld. When it was time for the Greek heroes or heroines to descend to the lower world, Persephone was there to guide, direct, and comfort them.

As a young innocent maiden, Persephone archetypically represents an unformed psyche, a girl who is influenced by family traditions, conventional religious beliefs of her culture, and societal expectations. Partially due to her extremely codependent relationship with her mother, Persephone is conditioned not to act from her deep core, as she has not developed a deep core or, to use Jungian psychology terms, individuated. Persephone tends to be malleable in nature and very passive, much the pleaser. She seems to remain in a state of chronic waiting – for someone to come along and "save" or transform her.

To become individuated, it was necessary for Persephone to descend into the underworld – into the "dark night of her soul." Because most people find it too terrifying to move into the world of the deep unconscious, they are usually "abducted" into it by a major life event – illness, death, divorce, or an enormous loss. Because the pain cracks through the carefully constructed protective defenses, they are forced to deal with it, just as Persephone did.

Persephone becomes a complete person, transformed by her trauma. She has tread the minefields of the deeper layers of the psyche, where the collective unconscious, feelings, deepest instincts, and knowing have been buried by centuries of patriarchal conditioning. As master of the underworld, the archetypal energy of Persephone is able to move fluidly between the everyday world and the depths of the unconscious, integrating both aspects comfortably into her being.

If the archetypal aspect of Persephone is pulled into the unconscious world with no guide, the result can be a break with reality – and the energy becomes "imprisoned" in the form of depression or psychosis. Because of the modern focus on the external world, and the move away from mythological symbolism, there seems a mass epidemic of emotional problems. The Persephone myth represents what happens when a woman falls into a serious depression. It is usually a result of subscribing to the societal tenets on the ideal woman – passive and pleasing. The undeveloped Persephone archetypal energy holds her anger in, as she does not want to face rejection by showing her anger. Her withheld feelings fold inward, resulting in depression. Depression is a separation from life and spirit, a symptom requiring change – a change to move beyond the lack of personal power, the inability to "see" beyond the five senses of the world.

The underworld is one of symbols, intuition, and receptivity. A nurturing and acceptance of the self is of utmost importance in healing the wounds of the psyche. The recording of dreams and individual meaning ascribed are an important part of this process. The eight hours a day spent in sleep are roughly equivalent to the one-third of the time Persephone spent in the underworld. The restorative dream time during sleep allows symbols and stories to play out in our psyche, imbuing us with the opportunity to heal and become whole. The rich symbolism and messages should be honored and our dreams nourished and cultivated.

The book *Alice in Wonderland* vividly reflects the Persephone myth. It is a story of innocence, loss, and ultimately wisdom and transformation. When

Persephone

Persephone, as Alice, goes to the underworld, she unites with masculine energy, strengthens the feminine, and brings back these qualities to the world. Because of the alchemical change, she is never the same. She is wise now and knows the value and necessity of the underworld – that of the mystical, magical, and intuitive, and brings it back to the common world to help others find their way.

Persephone also represents Eve in the Garden of Eden. Eve is naive and innocent before she takes a bite of the red apple. By eating of the red apple she becomes aware of the polarities of good and evil. The harmony and innocence of her world is now divided. Her journey of life becomes a journey back to balance and harmony – not an innocent harmony but a wise and consciously chosen harmony – and becomes a threat to the masculine power structure. Without the conscious harmonization of both masculine and feminine energies, we cannot re-enter the gates of Eden.

The skewing of society from patriarchal intervention has been party to keeping female energy contained and limited – so it does not become a threat to the masculine power structure.

Demeter

CHAMBER: Second/orange
Goddess of the second chamber/abdomen
SYMBOL: Mysteries of Eleusis, single ear of corn,
ear of barley, sheaf of wheat, earth mother,
lady of the plants, fruit, flower, seed, torch
DESCRIPTION: Tall, radiantly beautiful, unadorned,
unaffected, slender ankles

DEMETER is the consummate "earth mother" and goddess of agriculture. She is in charge of reproduction and the renewal of life. She loves to be surrounded by children and always seems to have a baby on her hip while she tends to the plants and fields. She loves to cook and enjoys preparing nutritious meals for her family and friends, putting her soul into every dish she makes.

Not only is she a wonderful nurturer, but she is a great listener and gives deeply thoughtful feedback to those who are experiencing emotional pain. People are embraced in warmth and love, just by being in her presence.

Demeter is very much a homebody, and is instinctually immersed in creating a homey, inviting environment for her family. If Demeter does not experience a solid Demeter role model from her mother in her formative years, she will draw on the mother within to provide her soul with that nourishment of mothering.

Demeter is attractive in an unadorned, non-egotistical, unselfconscious way. She attracts grounded, practical, and sensible men. This fits her desire for a mate who is reliable and solid – a good father for her children who won't wander too far from the nest.

Demeter's Mysteries were celebrated at her temple in Eleusis, built over a sacred well, for two thousand years. (The well was thought to be a portal for the life force of the Sophia energy. Geomagnetic earth energy appears to flow abundantly from these areas.) Demeter was the "Queen" and led the annual pilgrim celebrations for nine days. The content of the ceremonies were deep, guarded secrets.

Every new initiate was required to walk the sacred road, and cross a narrow bridge that is still evident today in the area near Athens, Greece. The area was considered sacred because it was the realm of departed spirits, representing the space between the worlds of the living and the dead. The pilgrims' walk was symbolic of the hero's difficult journey. People of all classes participated in the ceremonies. The requirements were: knowledge of the Greek language; fees for the priests, priestesses, and guides; a sacrificial pig; and a month's wage.

Each aspect of the journey reenacted a part of the ancient story of Demeter and Persephone. The initiates summoned Persephone back from the dead as they walked and called upon the spirit of Dionysus, god of inebriants, to guide them. Upon arrival at Eleusis, they danced all night around the well where Demeter had mourned for her lost daughter. All the universal elements sprang to life and joined them in their celebration. Only after they passed through the fortress wall gates was the great Mystery of Eleusis enacted.

What occurred inside the temple was a secret, the revelation of which was punishable by death. The part that could be revealed was the fact that the initiates experienced an awesome vision, transforming them forever. The essence of the Mystery Event was the sacred marriage, and the consummate joining.

When Persephone is in the underworld, she takes the pomegranate seed into her own body, ensuring the continuity of the life cycle – birth, death, resurrection, and redemption. The sign of redemption was an ear of barley, the risen grain, to be planted and produced again and again.

Demeter is the great mother and the world is her child, Persephone. The Mystery celebrations were healing events, the balm of which is the experience that there is no death – that all life returns to life. Rebirth from death, and the initiates' actual experience as such, was the secret of Eleusis.

Persephone and Demeter, during the great Mystery celebrations, bring us back to embrace those long-suppressed archetypes within ourselves: the earth as sacred, our mother, and balanced with the divine feminine as well as the masculine.

Hecate

Support goddess for Demeter and Artemis
Goddess of the dark side of the moon
SYMBOL: Dark moon
Destroyer of the old, elixir of the new

HECATE is the support goddess of Persephone and Demeter, a goddess of wise magic and crossroads. She is a little-known or honored archetype of the mother goddess, yet her energy is essential in the negotiation of the underworld and the world of everyday. Hecate was present at the abduction of Persephone into the underworld. She is a navigator who bridges the dark and light sides of Persephone and allows her to traverse and balance those two worlds.

During the Mysteries of Eleusinia in Greece, Hecate was one part of the triple goddess – Persephone, Demeter, and Hecate. Hecate was instrumental in negotiating the form of reunion for Persephone and Demeter – the incorporation of the old and the new for transformation – for something new and better. Hecate's energy served as the elixir in the alchemical blend of the Demeter and Persephone energies.

Hestia

CHAMBER: Third/yellow
Goddess of the hearth and home
Goddess of the third chamber/solar plexus
SYMBOL: Sun

HESTIA is the archetype of the sacred fire of the hearth, a guard of the eternal flame that burns at the center of the soul. She is essential to the emotional health of the modern-day woman – as she balances the energy of the soul and therefore life itself.

Hestia's archetype is an independent, introverted energy that focuses on the need to have a safe place to reside, that home is one's castle, and the central station of life itself. If home is honored, life tends to remain calm, even though winds and torrential rain can be whipping around it – the center stays strong and the flame of the hearth burns steadily.

In mythology, Hestia is the goddess of the hearth, a virgin goddess, keeper of the home fires and a symbol of the home. The newborn child was to be carried before Hestia before the child could be received into the family. It was to Hestia that every meal prayer or offering was made.

In ancient Greece, each city had a public hearth where the fire offered to Hestia was never to go out – the eternal flame. From this fire, coals were carried to a new colony. In Rome, six virgin priestesses called Vestals cared for the fire.

Hestia's task is to tend the fire. Fire itself is a dichotomy and contradiction as it brings warmth – and destruction. Fire brings desire as in passion. In her solitude, in the presence of fire, Hestia is not necessarily in a calm place. Desire can be unpleasant, uncomfortable, a fire raging out of control. Fire and desire create change.

Being in the Hestia place makes one feel fire with the body; feel more *in* the body. Fire is in constant motion. When one has not dealt effectively with the Hestia center, the result can be unresolved anger, the repression of passion for life or a person, and a feeling ineffectuality, and lack of personal regard. A positive relationship with Hestia allows an individual to develop a positive self-regard that comes from dealing effectively with desires.

Hera

In ancient Greece, **HERA** is goddess of marriage, a relationship archetype, a queen goddess. Her energy loves to command and rule, whether it be in the form of family, friends, organizations, and clubs – but always in conjunction with masculine energy as the primary power. She derives her power by association with masculine energy, usually in conjunction with her life partner.

As the Queen of Olympus in Greek mythology, Hera was the primary female goddess, by virtue of her marriage to Zeus. This is a reflection of the change in status from a matriarchal to patriarchal culture. Thousands of years before, of which ancient cave art attests, the female body was worshipped as part of fertility rite. The female body was a sign of creativity and productivity.

Hera was a powerful representation of this earlier reverence, and was often associated with spiritual symbols – birds, snakes, and products of the earth. The great power was considered feminine, as represented by woman, who had the power to produce life.

In ancient Greece, the most ancient of temples were dedicated to Hera, as representative of the divine feminine.

Hera is often manifested as the family matriarch, surrounded by her husband, and hoards of children and grandchildren at her feet. She is very sensitive to her position in society.

Athena

CHAMBER: Blue chamber
Goddess of wisdom
Goddess of the fifth chamber/throat
SYMBOL: Sword, armor

Born to a father only, **ATHENA** lives in her head. The myth of Athena's birth gives mention that her biological mother was Metis, (a Greek word for "wisdom,") a pre-Olympian Titan suppressed by the later patriarchy. Zeus swallowed Metis for two reasons: to ensure that she would not have a son who could threaten his position and so that Metis' wisdom would become a part of Zeus. This began the psychological warfare of male energy with his innate feminine (anima).

When Zeus "swallowed" Metis, he also removed from the world the matriarchal society norms, the times before patriarch-dominated society. The removal and subsequent repression of this "wisdom" energy is what the Eleusinian Mysteries celebrated to ensure the continuation of: the eternal and mystical cycle of birth and death, redemption, restoration, transformation, and wholeness. Because Athena has been guided by the patriarchal/father principle only, she is deeply in need of the warmth and unconditional love of mother/Demeter.

A modern woman in whom the Athena archetype is dominant will most likely identify with her ego – her place in the world, business, and intellectual acumen and worldly success as defined by the masculine. Her energy is locked into the fixed mode of consciousness. Her task is to open the closed vault of her intellect and connect with the lower rooms – particularly with the second chamber, in which mother/Demeter rules.

Athena's biggest task, as her symbols of sword and armor represent, is breaking through her fortress of defense mechanisms to allow for the free flow of energy through her being – to open the doors to all the chambers to allow for a healthy and balanced exchange of energy.

Artemis

CHAMBER: Sixth/purple
Goddess of the moon and hunt
Goddess of the sixth chamber/third eye
SYMBOL: The Arrow

ARTEMIS is the independent goddess of the hunt and moon. She is the independent archetype of the pure and primitive, the "wild woman" of the spirit. Artemis represents solitude and deep connection with nature and wildlife.

Artemis is renowned for her laser-focused goal setting. Her twin brother is Apollo. Artemis is known for her many accomplishments and as a protector and confidant to female friends. In contemporary life, she is seen as a supreme athlete – the ultimate marathon runner. Artemis does not identify with motherhood or sensuality or attaching to a male figure for identification. She is one unto herself. The Artemis archetype has usually struck the chord within herself by finding the balance of her masculine and feminine within. Therefore, she is not compelled to go in "search" of the masculine in the form of a male figure, to complete herself.

The Artemis archetype's task is to open to the other chambers within and draw from them to have an enriched feminine energy within.

Aphrodite

CHAMBER: Seventh/gold-silver
Goddess of beauty and love
Goddess of the seventh chamber
SYMBOL: Interlocking Hearts

APHRODITE is both an independent and dependent goddess – indulgent in the world of the physical to enhance her spiritual nature. Aphrodite holds her sexuality as a sacred gift to be used in reverence to God. She also bestows a wonder upon the art forms of painting, sculpture, music, and poetry. She thrives in gratification of the sensual pleasures. Aphrodite excels in the quality of being connected – of connecting heaven and earth.

Aphrodite is also a goddess of compassion who has grown into wisdom by her many trials, tribulations, sufferings, and broken heart. She is the goddess of the heart – symbolizing the ability to feel deeply, and with abandonment, the full range of emotions of life: joy and sorrow, pain and loss, as well as boundless joy and passion. Her heart symbolizes the authenticity and truth of our deepest well of self – unadorned and vulnerable. She allows two hearts to join in harmony with the powerful impact of the joining of the physical, the closest experience to heaven one will find in this world.

Aphrodite is the goddess of love and beauty, an alchemical goddess, incorporating all the elements and that of the sensual to culminate in the sacred marriage, the perfect balance of the masculine and feminine to achieve union with the divine energy.

The First Chamber

The Sacral/Root Center

SPIRITUAL ARMOR: The word of God
SYMBOL: Shoes "fitted with readiness of the word" for firm walk in the world
COLOR: Red
PURPOSE: Sense of grounding and place in the world based on family, religion, country, culture
DEADLY SIN: Sloth, or refusal to do the essential soul work
MEDITATION: On sacral area (tailbone) – send red energy through body areas, igniting the fire of life, the torch of the spirit, the baptism by fire
FRUIT OF THE SPIRIT: Patience
GODDESS: Persephone – innocent maiden
CHARACTERISTICS: Introverted, sensation oriented
POSITIVE TRAITS: Receptive, imaginative, dreamer, psychic abilities
NEGATIVE TRAITS: Depression oriented, can be manipulated, manipulative, withdrawal into unreality, psychotic break
NEGATIVE PHYSICAL MANIFESTATIONS: Physical suffering in the legs, lower body parts, chronic pain in feet and general aches. Many cannot release the toxins in their body through elimination so they suffer in their bowels. Immune system is not working adequately to ward off germs and viruses that invade the body.
THE SYMBOL: The armor is used when Eva undergoes a knighting ritual during her time in the first chamber of the castle. The shield of the leather lace-up shoes is bestowed upon Eva by the Knight, as a "grounding force" and shield of defense, a protection for her spiritual life. Thick leather shields were often used by medieval knights. Even to this day, popes and bishops have maintained the symbolism of the shield: symbols that reveal their theology and spirituality. Pope John Paul II declared his devotion to the Eucharist, to Mary, evidenced by the symbol on his shield.

FIRST CHAMBER MEDITATION

Monday – Persephone Day

I feel connected to the earth. The universal energy pours down through the crown of my head to the soles of my feet, and into the roots of the earth as I exhale. As I inhale I feel the tingling energy of the earth penetrate the soles of my feet, the warmth effusing throughout my body, bringing all my senses to life. I am being reborn into my life here on earth. My life force is returning in abundance. My heart swells with gratitude, and I feel the warmth penetrating every cell, every organ of my physical body, strengthening my support skeleton: my hip bones, my legs, my feet, my immune system. I bask in the heat of the red light of the first chamber, and savor its warmth. I am energized, I am patient, and my feet are fitted with the shoes of readiness to walk in the world.

I draw on the energy of the goddess Persephone, on her innocence, her depth, her dives into the murky waters of the subconscious, unafraid to reveal and examine what she finds within. I allow her full reign in my imagination, and respect her energies. Mondays are Persephone days – the days that I will dress in red and set up an altar cloaked in red lace to honor her archetype and resolve to keep her strong as part of the necessary balance within myself.

The Second Chamber

The Abdominal Center

SPIRITUAL ARMOR: Prayer
SYMBOL: Praying hands
COLOR: Orange
PURPOSE: One-on-one relationships
DEADLY SIN: Lust, feeling of lack, ungrounded, spiritual dearth
MEDITATION: Abdominal area, sexual organs, creativity
FRUIT OF THE SPIRIT: Kindness
GODDESS: Demeter – mother, great mother
CHARACTERISTICS: Extraverted, feeling, nurturing
POSITIVE TRAITS: Maternal, nurturing, generous
NEGATIVE TRAITS: Depression, burnout, fosters dependency, unplanned pregnancy
NEGATIVE PHYSICAL MANIFESTATIONS: Physical dysfunctions in the form of back pain, sciatica nerve problems, vaginal infections, endometriosis, infertility, depression, sexual potency and desire, urinary tract infections, fibroids caused from inhibited creativity, and prostate problems.
SYMBOL: Praying hands – hands are used to physically communicate our intentions. We can use our hands to invite, beckon, reject, console, protect, embrace, or soothe. We use our hands to work, touch, hurt, or heal our wounds and those of loved ones. When we pray, we focus our attention and bring our hands together to en-flesh the sacred. Prayer is recognized physically through our hand position.

In this chamber, Eva prays with her hands clasped together. The "praying hands" originated in the feudal system for the knights. In this way, the hands come together to exchange energy between the right and left sides of our physical form. When a knight is dubbed, they are encased by the hands of his lord. In this way the lord symbolically imparts his authority, his acceptance and his blessings.

SECOND CHAMBER MEDITATION

Tuesday – Demeter Day

I draw on the power of the topaz. I am a creator, electrically and magnetically alive, and connected with the universe. I feel my orange energy emanating from my abdominal center out into the world. I connect the strands of energy to those I love. I radiate love to them and lift them up. I know that each person in my life is here for a reason, even those who have harmed me have been my greatest teachers. I send kindness to them. I am grateful to those lessons and their role in my spiritual development. I now mentally unplug the circuits to those people, as I choose not to receive their negative energy. I only choose to send my positive energy to them, then disconnect those circuits. I am grateful for the loving relationships in my life, and I allow only love to fill the second room of my castle.

Today I honor Demeter, the maternal goddess archetype and goddess of the grain, a nurturing relationship energy. I construct an altar to Demeter, valuing her abundant qualities of giving. I place a carved statue of Mary and the baby Jesus in the center of the altar. I enjoy cooking for my family and doing for others in a quiet way. I allow the Demeter energy to nurture the other archetypal energies within myself, even those that seem to require nurturing – such as Hestia, Athena, and Artemis.

The Third Chamber

The Solar Plexus Center

SPIRITUAL ARMOR: Faith
SYMBOL: Shield of faith
COLOR: Yellow
PURPOSE: Self-esteem, ego versus the higher self, ability to be successful in this world, willing to risk everything for what you know to be true.
DEADLY SIN: Unresolved anger
MEDITATION: Solar plexus, beginning of intuitive learning/knowing/trusting
FRUIT OF THE SPIRIT: Discipline, self-control, containment of the ego, allowing the ego to serve as structure for operating from the higher self
GODDESS: Hestia – goddess of the hearth, keeps the fire burning
CHARACTERISTICS: Introverted, feeling, intuitive
POSITIVE TRAITS: Enjoys solitude, sense of spiritual meaning
NEGATIVE TRAITS: Emotional distance, lack of social persona, loves to stay home.
Negative physical manifestations: Some of the physical problems people experience when they stay stuck in the ego and refuse to work the third chamber are chronic pain in the form of ulcers, indigestion, anorexia, bullimia, elevated blood sugar, stress-related incontinence, and general malaise from toxic waste.
SYMBOL: Fire at the banquet table, fire that burns at the center of the soul of every human being

THIRD CHAMBER MEDITATION

Wednesday – Hestia Day

The warmth of the bright yellow fills my solar plexus between my abdomen and my chest. Liquid sun flows up to my heart, bathing it in a loving, brilliant light. It slowly moves to my heart, softening it, melting it, as I feel an expansion and opening. I stay with the energy and follow it upward through the neck as it slowly spreads its joy, massaging my face muscles as I relax completely and bask in the glow. The yellow trail moves to the third eye, sharing its special energy, then travels to the crown of my head where it blends with the white light, then travels back down my spine, circling around each vertebra, then bathes my feet and journeys back up to home in the third room. The yellow light slowly congeals into the fruit of discipline, magnetizing my energy into a focused beam of light to accomplish the task at hand.

I honor the archetypal energies of Hestia, independent virgin goddess of the home and hearth. I value her spiritual fire that burns at the center of my being, knowing that I can go to this safe place of restoration anytime. I recognize the wise spirit of Hestia within and turn to her for solace and strength. She is the still point in the center of the wheel, the calm flame that keeps burning when chaos is raging around her. I build a hearth, an altar, in the middle of my house and spirit for Hestia, where her flame keeps burning. The Hestia in me does not seek crowds, notoriety, or drama. She likes to care for the home, the spirit, making it the nicest dwelling place it can be.

Wednesday I keep for Hestia day. The kitchen and hearth are places in the home where her spirit burns the strongest. I light a candle on the yellow altar and place a picture of sunflowers next to it. I honor her archetype within myself and think of her quiet core throughout the day.

The Fourth Chamber

The Heart Center

SPIRITUAL ARMOR: Righteousness
SYMBOL: Breastplate of righteousness
COLOR: Green, laced with pink
PURPOSE: Understanding love
DEADLY SIN: Gluttony, devouring, excessive behaviors and patterns
MEDITATION: Heart and chest area, allowing flow as opposed to "taking in"
FRUIT OF THE SPIRIT: Abundant love
GODDESS: Hera – queen of hearts, wife of Zeus, goddess of marriage
CHARACTERISTICS: Extraverted, feeling, sensation
POSITIVE TRAITS: Ability to make lifetime commitment, fidelity
NEGATIVE TRAITS: Jealousy, vindictiveness, rage, inability to leave destructive relationships
NEGATIVE PHYSICAL MANIFESTATIONS: Pain and symptoms in shoulders and arms, chest, ribs, and breast tissues, in the diaphragm, and thymus gland. Physical dysfunctions that can manifest from dis-ease in these areas are heart dis-ease, mitral valve prolapse, upper back and shoulder pain, chronic bronchitis, palpitations, panic disorders.
SYMBOL: Breastplate of armor – the breastplate was used in medieval times as a form of protection, just as the heart needs the spiritual protection of the white light.

FOURTH CHAMBER MEDITATION

Thursday – Hera Day

The green light is the most powerful energy in the universe, and I remember this as I open my heart and send the green glow through my body, loving and nurturing every cell as it goes, wrapping its green love and light in an embrace around everything in its path. The green energy reminds me of the incredible miracle of our existence and the wonderful opportunity to experience and make a difference in the universe during our sojourn on this earth plane. Every cell is bathed in love, and I feel calm, deeply relaxed, and centered.

In the green light of love, I forgive those who have harmed me and forgive myself for the harm I have done to others. I let go of any guilt I feel over any past experiences. I have incorporated these experiences as part of my life lessons, and I have made restitution. I will not punish myself by carrying the baggage. As I breathe out, I let go of any residue; release it with my breath. I breathe in the fresh, clean oxygen of new beginnings. I feel complete. I feel whole. I give love with the release of my next breath and enjoy watching the green-pink light circle out into the world. I breathe in the vast unending universal love, feeling it surge through my veins and massage all the organs of my body.

I watch the goddess Hera, the feminine archetype of marriage, glide into the room. I see love pouring from her heart and the glow in her eyes as she prepares the chamber for her beloved. She knows the value of opening to another human being and how their energies enrich and expand as a couple. They are much more effective together than they can ever be alone – they represent the perfect complement and balance of the masculine and feminine energies. Knowing that the marriage of a male and female deeply in love is a metaphor for that perfect balance of the masculine and feminine energies within, and it is well worth striving for. She knows the meaning of vulnerability, of risk, in opening herself to an intimate relationship. Hera is not afraid to love because her other goddess energies are strong, and will carry her when she is wounded.

The Fifth Chamber

The Throat Center

SPIRITUAL ARMOR: Truth

SYMBOL: Belt of truth

COLOR: Cobalt blue

PURPOSE: Will/expression/truth/discernment

DEADLY SIN: Envy, a feeling of lack precedes envy, wanting something someone else has that you haven't "done the work" to acquire. This can be manifested in the desire to naturally express the authentic self.

MEDITATION: To find your own truth, deeper truth, and trust it, allowing your actions in the world to be based on this truth, to discern God's will, the faith to receive it and act on it, even when personal ego's wants and desires are in opposition.

FRUIT OF THE SPIRIT: Faithfulness

GODDESS: Athena – goddess of intellect/wisdom. Athena is the goddess of wisdom and crafts, a virgin and warrior goddess – the protector, and was born, fully grown, from the head of Zeus. She is credited for making the olive tree – the most prized of all trees in Greece – grow in Athens.

CHARACTERISTICS: Extraverted, thinking, sensation

POSITIVE TRAITS: Thinks well on feet, speaks the truth, solves practical problems, strategic, trustworthy, trusting, sense of worthiness, forms strong alliance with men.

NEGATIVE TRAITS: Emotional distance, craftiness, lack of empathy, dishonest, manipulative

NEGATIVE MANIFESTATIONS: Pain in the muscles, tendons, and joints of the upper body, allergies, sinuses, raspy throat and loss of voice, adrenal glands, and temporal mandibular joint syndrome (TMJ).

SYMBOL: Belt of truth – the belt of truth symbolizes the importance of being truthful with ourselves and aware of every aspect of our being: our thoughts, ideas, attitudes, emotions, and energies. She identifies primarily with male energy and the patriarch.

FIFTH CHAMBER MEDITATION

Friday – Athena Day

The azure-blue energy is light and pure and communicates the importance of movement and change, and also faithfulness, transmitting that knowledge to every cell as it travels lightly up the throat to the third eye, then up over the head and down the spine. It slowly spirals back up the front of the body to rest in the throat once again. My mind is clear and focused so that I may listen to the perfect will of the creative energy flowing in abundance from the universe and informing me every second of my existence. I listen, I discern, and I act accordingly.

My reverence today is to Athena, goddess archetype of the fifth chamber. I honor and value the Athena within me; her intellect, wisdom, and courage to persevere for the truth. My Athena energy is the no-nonsense girl, practical, pragmatic, and efficient. She knows how to get things done and makes sure they're done effectively. I enjoy making things for the pleasure of it and also for the pleasure they bring to me when I look at or wear them. I get along well with male friends and they think of me as a "buddy." I love reading and studying and researching the past, traveling, and meeting people from other countries. I feel stable and balanced with a strong Athena working in me. She is independent and does not need a man to complete her identity.

I hum, chant, and sing as I focus my energy on Athena. I listen to the silence and the messages of truth that come through. I listen to my voice as it responds to my communication with the Athena energy. I am willing to communicate to the world the truth as it comes to me. Sometimes I just allow the sound to come from my throat as it will – and I listen. And I am thankful.

The Sixth Chamber

The Third Eye Center

SPIRITUAL ARMOR: Sword

SYMBOL: Sword of the spirit

COLOR: Purple – the Mediterranean sea snails of the Muricidae family where the dark wine-red color originated as royal purple. This color was limited to the royal family's use because the dye was difficult to obtain. Purple is also associated with excellence and with the hierarchy in academia. Here the doctoral hood is lined with purple fabric. In the *New Testament* we find Lydia, who was the "seller of purple." As a businesswoman, she was one of the most successful and influential woman in Phillipi. She sought truth and became one of Europe's first converts. Eva also recognizes that she is a seeker of truth in this chamber. Her arrival in the purple chamber is an accomplishment for her on her spiritual journey.

PURPOSE: Wisdom/knowing

DEADLY SIN: Pride/vainglory, intellectual hubris, knowledge used for one's own selfish aim rather than enhancement of the spirit and the world, "acting as God."

MEDITATION: A look through the lens of the left eye (male, structure, separateness, organization) and through the right eye (feminine, intuitive, life force, flow, creativity, nurturing) and finally to a combination of both, creating balance, wisdom

FRUIT OF THE SPIRIT: Peace

GODDESS: Artemis – goddess of the hunt/moon

CHARACTERISTICS: Extraverted, intuitive, feeling, strong sense of knowing the head energy and heart energy are connected and work as one

POSITIVE TRAITS: Sets and reaches goals, independence, autonomy, deep friendships

NEGATIVE TRAITS: Dependence, create their own reality

NEGATIVE MANIFESTATIONS: Headache pain, anxiety, ringing in the ears, rash, blurred vision, dizziness.

SYMBOL: The sword represents the ability to develop facilities via the "inner eye." During the course of spiritual maturation, the soul must develop the ability to use the left and right brain to see the whole picture, the trueness and richness of things. Some Westerners dismiss the importance of the inner eye, the third eye, or the center of wisdom. In some of the Eastern religions it is called the brow chakra.

In Eva's story, the sword is associated with the word of God. With the sword, Eva is able to discern the truth in the world around her and combine it with her knowledge of the truth of her own being.

SIXTH CHAMBER MEDITATION

Saturday – Artemis Day

The purple light coursing through my system represents the energy of strength, of perfect balance, as it blends with the pure white light of the universe, which courses through the top of my head. I want for nothing and need nothing else at this moment but the perfect balance of my masculine and feminine energies. There is nothing I need that the universe will not provide for me. In this room I let go of my attachments, my compulsions, my doubts, and my fears. In this room I surrender my all to the universal energy, nearing purification as I near the white light. I feel perfect peace.

Today is Saturday, the day to honor the goddess energies of Artemis, independent goddess of the moon and hunt. I honor her energy within and feel her strength as I set solid goals, and defend what is true and right in the world. I appreciate her ability to see by moonlight – to "see in the dark" – and act on what she sees. I love nothing more than being out in nature – in the forest and fields, out on the sea, and in the mountains. I feel a deep connection with the universe, and everything in it, when I'm close to nature and recognize the Artemis energy in me.

The Seventh Chamber

The Crown Center

COLOR: Pure white/gold/silver

SPIRITUAL ARMOR: Crown

SYMBOL: Helmet of salvation

PURPOSE: The perfect balance of the masculine and feminine energy within uniting with the universal energy of the divine, the "sacred marriage" or *heiros gamos.*

DEADLY SIN: Greed, wanting it all, expansive.

MEDITATION: A walk through the labyrinth – to the Holy Grail center.

FRUIT OF THE SPIRIT: Perfect joy

GODDESS: Aphrodite – goddess of love

CHARACTERISTICS: Extraverted, sensation,

POSITIVE TRAITS: Pleasure-oriented, appreciates beauty, sensuous nature, creative, able to be in the moment, magnanimous, receptive, quiet strength

NEGATIVE TRAITS: Serial relationships, promiscuity, difficulty considering consequences, impulsive, addiction prone, lacks discernment, complacent

NEGATIVE PHYSICAL MANIFESTATIONS: Depression, fatigue, sleep dysfunction, insomnia, increased weight, sexual dysfunction

SYMBOL: The helmet of salvation represents the anointing and opening of the crown chakra, to allow the universal divine energy to pour into crown of the head

SEVENTH CHAMBER MEDITATION

Sunday – Aphrodite Day

I float on beds of puffy white cloud, far above the earth, breathing in the white light of the divine energy. I breathe in and exhale, just as the ocean breathes in the salty water, then exhales, sending it back to the sands. My breath feels like the rhythm of the tides, the sea water within, ebbing and flowing. I listen only to the rhythm of my own breath, and think of the seas, the emerald color of the water, the sun glistening like diamonds on the waves, and the dolphins dancing happily near the shore.

This is the room of the union of the balance of the sacred masculine and the sacred feminine with the divine universal energy of that of God. I move with the white light, ride it like a magic carpet as it soars through my body, connecting me with *all that is*. I am one with everything and everything is part of me. I am strong, because the greatest force in the universe is with me, is within me. I am joyful. And I am made whole.

Sunday is Aphrodite day, the goddess archetype of love and beauty. I honor the beautiful, sensual, graceful nature of the Aphrodite within me, the flow of her pure energy. Her sacred archetype, embodied in a carved wooden statue, holds a reverential place in my home. I feel her vibrant white energy flowing through me, and she is a conductor of the connection between the human and divine. She is independent, free, relational, stable, and yet ever changing. When the Aphrodite energy is strong I connect deeply with both spirit and humanity, and find that I am a strong presence wherever I go. I take in the universal Aphrodite energy as I breathe in, sending it into the world as I exhale.

Theological Reflection

ST. TERESA OF AVILA was the first woman to be given the title, "Doctor of the Church," awarded by the institution in which she offered her many gifts. She was a religious reformer, spiritual director, and author of multiple manuscripts on prayer and the spiritual journey. Classics endure the test of time, and her writings are still in print over four hundred years later. On one level she wrote through the lens of her deep prayer life, which was conditioned by physical disabilities, the loss of her mother as a teenager, and the residue of anti-Semitism launched against her grandfather. On another level, her writing style is characterized by vivid, medieval images, as evidenced in her most famous work, *The Interior Castle*, published in 1588.

Beyond the Castle Doors follows the structure of the seven mansions of Teresa's *Interior Castle*. The work, however, translates Teresa's language and metaphors into story, a blend of the medieval with the present culture, which better speaks to the modern woman. A knight functions as an angel, a messenger from God, to guide Eva through the castle.

In Teresa's original work, a soul enters a castle, seemingly guided by a divine spirit, though the second party is implied. Later, she names her guide as mental prayer. The outside of the castle has the aura of a hostile environment. The inside has seven dwelling places. The center room, the seventh room, is the most desired, the most beautiful, and offers the most intense experience of God. She describes the variations of mental prayer, the gateway, which help her proceed through the seven rooms.

In the first "chamber," one begins to pray, but is unable to give total focus to God, due to the interference of the hostile environment outside. These are the noisy distractions of what Teresa calls "worldly influences," translated into modern terms as an excess of commercialism, materialism, and over-commitment. For Eva, it is infidelity, the weakness of not being true to one's self. Sin leaves one hollow, empty, longing for a deeper connection to God. In an earlier work, *The Way of Perfection,* Teresa spoke of the need for purgation. One must purge oneself of time spent on the meaningless, the hollow, and replace that time with loftier activities.

In the second "chamber," one's personal relationship with God begins. Teresa recognizes God's call in sermons, spiritual books, wisdom figures, illnesses, and trials. The first attempts at prayer are rewarded, and one can more sharply hear God's call. This is the stage of preparation. It could be compared to the modern woman's honeymoon, or relational stage to her spouse. In the beginning, sacrifices for the beloved are overlooked and love-making is rewarding. Medieval nuns, though remaining celibate, went through a period of novitiate or apprenticeship when consolations in prayer were the norm, perhaps as God's gift of encouragement, or perhaps because the experiences were fresh.

The third "chamber" is a place of settling down. A person lives a well-balanced life and reaches out to help others. But one can be seduced by the tranquility. Control itself can become an attachment. The object of this stage is conformity with God's will, not our desire of consolation or delight. Gradually, one learns what God wants. To grow, one must become detached from security, from a need to control. One must willfully embrace insecurity.

The fourth "chamber" calls one to a more passive, almost effortless prayer. One does not need order and control. Rather, one has a lively faith and freedom in the service of God. Prayer is instinctive. Teresa here offers the famous image of the two ways of filling a fountain. One can laboriously pull up water from a distant well and transport it by aqueduct to the fountain. Or one can build a fountain over the source of the water, allowing the fountain to fill effortlessly from within. Our efforts at prayer (stage three) might be called meditation. Our effortless prayer (stage four) might be termed contemplation. In theological language, the latter is God's gratuitous grace, pure gift. Meditation can be worked at. It sets the stage for contemplation, that which is to come… Effortless prayer (stage four) is termed contemplation. In theological language, the latter is God's gratuitous grace, pure gift. In human terms, one can offer gifts to one's lover, but one cannot program the response.

Teresa was revolted by the idea that one type of prayer supersedes another. One needs all of the "chambers" at different times of one's life. One needs meditation of the sacred scriptures, intentional *lexio divina* or divine reading, the ritual life in the sacraments of the Church, and one needs to set aside time where contemplative prayer can happen.

Deep contemplative prayer happens in the fifth "chamber." The rapture is described as a soul in suspension. It is captured in the artist Bernini's famous sculpture of St. Teresa being pierced by an angel. But one cannot simulate it on one's own efforts. She uses the metaphor of a silkworm. One's spiritual journey goes through the stages of a metamorphosis like the butterfly, which must pass through the stages of a caterpillar and a cocoon. In Christian theology, the historical Jesus died, had fallow time in the tomb or cocoon, and was reborn as the Christ figure. Those on the spiritual path hope to imitate Christ in this pattern.

In Teresa's earlier work, *The Way of Perfection,* she uses the language of purgation, illumination, and union. In the letting go or death stage, one's sins, limitations, and weaknesses press in and undermine one's sense of self-worth. The soul is suffocated by anxiety and bitterness. Prayer is next to impossible. Teresa's spiritual director, John of the Cross, coined this stage *The Dark Night of the Soul,* and wrote his own journey under this title.

In Teresa's fifth room in the *Interior Castle,* the Spouse (God) makes the soul desire (God) vehemently by certain delicate means, which the soul itself does not understand. These impulses are so refined that Teresa is unable to put them into words.

The sixth "chamber" is a place for intense union with God. It builds upon the fourth and fifth dwelling places. It is here that Teresa compares the mystical phenomena to fire in her heart. Both the pain and the joy are intense. She calls this stage a spiritual marriage with God. It is a total giving to God, but it needs replenishing. Dialogue with holy people, spiritual direction, retreats, sacramental confession, these can replenish the soul. She felt that everyone needed a spiritual companion. In this section she describes a kind of rapture in which the soul, even though not in prayer, is touched by some word it remembers or hears about God. The Lord joins the soul with himself, and no one external to the soul and God knows that this intense communication is happening. Lovers tend to have private jokes that delight them – verbal exchanges, which describe a past experience that only the two of them witnessed and understand.

Also in stage six is another kind of rapture, call it flight of the spirit, which is purely interior. It is so swift that one must have strength and courage if one is not to be frightened by it. In human terms, it happens to those who experience love at first sight. One needs a special trust not to be frightened by it. St. Paul in his conversion experience spoke of an experience that he could not say if he were in the body or out of the body.

In "chamber" seven the triune God took over the interior of Teresa's heart.

Theological Reflection

Rather than being oblivious to her surroundings, the soul is more attentive to all that belongs to the service of God. In human terms, the beloved is so secure in the love of her lover that she has thoughts of him in the back of her mind and longs for times to rest in the happy companionship of the other. Teresa has great confidence that God will not leave her, and that, having taken her to this chamber, God will not allow her to lose it.

Teresa speaks of a spiritual marriage in metaphorical language. The connection is so strong that God could reach the soul even though a stone wall separated them. Mechtild of Magdaberg would say, God comes to the soul, effortlessly, as dew descends upon the flower. This instantaneous communication of God to the soul is so sublime a favor, and such delight, that Teresa does not know with what to compare it, beyond saying that the Lord is pleased to manifest to the soul at that moment the glory that is in heaven... Then, Teresa goes on to describe the soul's response. The soul cannot help but utter words of intimacy such as those on the level of lovers in The Song of Songs.

Teresa does not shy away from giving her opinion on controversial Reformation topics, such as the controversy of faith versus faith with works. It is the theological issue of her era and she comes at it from the Catholic perspective. Virtues are to be practiced. If one does not go forward one begins to go back. The soul in love with God cannot be stagnant.

Thus, Teresa ends with saying that when one reaches the seventh mansion or "chamber," one has not really arrived. The spiritual journey is completed only when one moves from life into the noetic mysticism of the eternal.

The Holy Grail in this life is a glimpse into the wordlessness of eternal experience, with subtle clues strewn about as to the identification of the Grail. Eva's journey through the interior castle recapitulates St. Teresa's experience and establishes spiritual guideposts and markers for the reader's own soul journey. The result is a deepened life experience, a close, rich walk with God, and a life generated by a desire to serve both God and humankind – with love.

— *Carolyn Sur, SSND, PhD*

Afterword

SOPHIA ENERGY, simply put, is the feminine energy of God. One finds God's manifestations in feminine form in the Judeo-Christian scriptures, the *Torah*, which is accepted both by Judaism and Christianity. In the First Book of Genesis, the Hebrew language names God in action, God's energy, with a feminine noun, *Ruah*.

Genesis tells us in the first verse that a "breath" or "wind" from God swept over the waters of chaos, bringing order to the existing universe. Any woman who daily attempts to put order into her household can see herself in *Ruah*. Translation into English obscures *Ruah's* feminine context. God's action, according to some theological schools of thought, is equivalent to God's essence.

Thus, the feminine dimension of God's energy or "breath" was obvious to linguists in the pre-Christian era. The noun endings and the spelling of the article preceding the noun in some languages indicates the gender of the word, masculine or feminine or, in some languages, neuter.

Hebrew is one language whose nouns connote gender. A feminine name does not limit God to feminine actions, such as birthing and nursing, any more than the Latin term, *Deus*, validates that God's essence is limited to the realm of masculine concerns. Gender-specific language for God does effect the multiplicity of images for God and is suggestive of God's incomprehensibility. Language helps to keep the imagination open to God's many manifestations.

The Jews gradually came to use other terms for the Godhead, which suggested the feminine dimension. One such name was *Shekhinah*, but its interpretation was configured and reconfigured over the centuries. A single word seldom conveys all the particulars it is intended to explain. *Shekhinah* is derived from the Hebrew *shakan*, meaning presence or act of dwelling, and is expressed as a feminine gender substantive. Gloria L. Scwabb, SSJ, raised the *Shekhinah* notion to a new level in an award winning paper orally presented at the Catholic Theological Society, June 2001. The author agreed to share her research which may, by now, be published as part of her dissertation.[67]

Shekhinah as presence is implied in the pillar of fire by night and the cloud by day during the Exodus: "With a column of cloud you led them by day, and

Afterword

by night with a pillar of fire, To light the way of their journey, the way in which they must travel." Nehemiah 9: 12.[68]

By the 12th century, Jewish mystics, the Kabbalahs, were influential in northern Spain. The theme of the Kabbalah mystics was the attainment of a state of mystical union in which all boundaries separating the self from God were overcome.

This Kabbalistic philosophy would prevail in the geographic area where Teresa of Avila's grandfather was raised. She would write a spiritual classic, *The Interior Castle,* in which one on the spiritual journey draws closer and deeper into union with the divine. In one sense, Teresa's journey imitates the Kabbalistic cosmology. As Teresa's journey contracts more to the interior of the castle, Teresa herself draws closer into the ecstasy of God found in the seventh mansion.

Reference to the feminine or Sophia energy in the Godhead resurfaced later in the Book of Wisdom. Here, Wisdom (Sophia) is translated into the English language and addressed with feminine pronouns:

> "for Wisdom, the artificer of all, taught me. For in her is a
> spirit intelligent, holy, unique, Manifold, subtle, agile, clear,
> unstained, certain, Not baneful, loving the good, keen,
> unhampered, beneficent, kindly, Firm, secure, tranquil, all-
> powerful, all-seeing, And pervading all spirits, though they
> be intelligent, pure and very subtle.
>
> For Wisdom is mobile beyond all motion, and she pen-
> etrates and pervades all things by reason of her purity.
> For she is an aura of the might of God and a pure effusion
> of the glory of the Almightly; therefore nought that is sul-
> lied enters into her.
> For she is the refulgence of eternal light, the spotless mir-
> ror of the power of God, the image of his goodness."
>
> — *Wisdom 7:22-26*[69]

In primitive agricultural society, energy was related to the fruits of the earth. As the earth is the archetype of energy, for the earth gives life, so the woman was associated with energy, because she, too, carries life. Since DNA had not been discovered, the magic of life came to be associated with "earth magic" and termed "mother earth" or terra mater[70]. From earth magic the goddess image emerged.

Joseph Campbell traces the personification of the feminine God to the warrior God. It is feminine energy that gives birth to forms and nourishes forms. The goddess was the only visualized divinity at that time, as demonstrated by the hundreds of early European Neolithic figurines in the form of goddesses. (See The Power of Myth by Joseph Campbell, for further development of this thought.[71])

Eventually, the goddess image gave way to the male image of a warrior God, and the wisdom energy diminished in the consciousness of Western religious people. She was restored somewhat with the Virgin in the Roman Catholic tradition. Modern theologians hold that it would be more accurate to attribute some of Mary's honors to the Holy Spirit: "Seat of Wisdom", "Cause of our Joy", and "Comforter of the Afflicted". Had this devotion been associated with the trinity, one could better see "spirit energy" as the energy of God, as Sophia energy.

Western philosophers addressed energy as change or flux. Even before Socrates they attempted to understand the world by use of reason, without appealing to religion or revelation. Their constant question was, "What are things made of?" In the sixth century BCE, the physics had not sufficiently developed to lead to today's conclusion, that all things are reducible to energy. Heraclitus thought that all reality is best described as "in flux" or changing. He describes it as a unit of opposites.

Centuries later, psychologists would remind us that, at our core personality, we too, are a paradox of opposites. Our greatest strength is our greatest weakness in disguise. The great psychologist Carl G. Jung coined the term *anima*, the feminine energy that is part of the male psyche, and the *animus*, the masculine energy that is part of the female psyche. He describes those closed off or unattended, seemingly negative aspects of the psyche, the *shadow*. By bringing the aspects of the shadow from the subconscious to conscious awareness, one can begin the process of healing and balance – and move into wholeness and unity with God. Eva's journey through the interior castle is one woman's path to healing. Through the story the reader is able to understand Jungian language through symbol and the creative experience.

Namaste
Carolyn Sur, SSND, PhD.

Afterword

"When he established the heavens I was there,
when he marked out the vault over the face of the deep;
When he made firm the skies above,
when he fixed fast the foundations of the earth;
When he set for the sea its limit,
so that the waters should not transgress his command;
Then was I beside him as his craftsman,
and I was his delight day by day, Playing before him
all the while, playing on the surface of his earth;
and I found delight in the sons of men."

— *Proverbs 8:27-3*[72]

AUTHORS' BIOGRAPHIES

Maria O'Brien, M.Ed., is a Licensed Professional Counselor and Marriage and Family Therapist. She is in private practice as a psychotherapist using her strong background in Jungian psychology. She lives with her family in Shreveport, Louisiana.

Debi King McMartin, MA, is an author, screenwriter, and documentary film-maker. She lives with her family in Bossier City, Louisiana.

Debi and Maria will be conducting workshops throughout the United States in conjunction with *Beyond the Castle Doors: A Soul Quest for the Holy Grail*. Readers are invited to visit their website at: www.interiorcastlework.com

Endnotes

Bible quotations taken from:

The New American Bible, Saint Joseph Edition
(New York: Catholic Book Publishing Co., 1992, 1987, 1980, 1970),

1 Proverbs 8:27-31, p. 709, The Old Testament.
2 John 14:2-4, p. 168, The New Testament.
3 Ephesians 6:10-20, pp. 299, The New Testament.

PART I

4 Proverbs 8:1-6.
5 Baruch 3:20-23.
6 Wisdom 7:21-27, p. 756-757, The Old Testament.
7 Proverbs 8:19-21.
8 Proverbs 8:14-17.
9 Galations 6:7-8, p. 291, The New Testament.
10 John 8:31-32, p. 159, The New Testament.
11 1 Thessalonians 5:18, p. 317, New Testament.
12 Exodus 20:13, p. 78 Old Testament.
13 Sirach 6:30, p. 777, The Old Testament.
14 Luke 12:31, The New Testament.
15 Proverbs 4:8-9.
16 Sirach 24:9.
17 John 14:27, p. 168, The New Testament.

PART II

18 Jeremiah 44:16-18, The Old Testament.
19 Revelation 12:1, p. 398, The New Testament.
20 1 Corinthians 1:22-23, p. 245, The New Testament.
21 1 Corinthians 1:25, p. 245, The New Testament.
22 1 Corinthians 1:30.
23 1 Corinthians 2:6-8, p. 245, The New Testament
24 1 Corinthians 2:7.
25 Romans 16:25, p. 242, The New Testament.
26 Ephesians 3:9-12, p. 296, The New Testament.
27 Sirach 24:26-27, p. 794, The Old Testament.
28 Sirach 24:1-3, p. 793, The Old Testament.
29 Sirach 1:6-8, p. 772, The Old Testament.
30 Wisdom 9:17, p. 758, The Old Testament.
31 Sirach 6:23-25.

32 Wisdom 7:25, 756, The Old Testament.
33 Wisdom 7:27, 756-757, The Old Testament.
34 Proverbs 8:27-31, p. 709, The Old Testament.
35 Wisdom 7:10-11.
36 Sirach 1:14, p. 772, The Old Testament.
37 Sirach 1:4, p. 772, The Old Testament.
38 Proverbs 8:22, p. 8:22, The Old Testament.
39 Baruch 3:29-32, p. 967, The Old Testament.
40 Proverbs 4:1-6, p. 705, The Old Testament.
41 Proverbs 4:13.
42 Proverbs 4:7-9, p. 705, The Old Testament.
43 Wisdom 7:24, p. 756, The Old Testament.
44 Wisdom 6:12-16, p. 755, The Old Testament.
45 Proverbs 1:20-23, p. 702, The Old Testament.
46 Proverbs 8:1-11, p. 708-709, The Old Testament.
47 Wisdom 9:10, P. 758, The Old Testament.
48 Wisdom 9:14-15, P. 758, The Old Testament.
49 Proverbs 8:18, P. 709, The Old Testament.
50 Sirach 1:17, P. 772, The Old Testament.
51 Proverbs 4:5-8, P. 705, The Old Testament.
52 Wisdom 8:3, P. 757, The Old Testament.
53 Wisdom 8:5, P. 757, The Old Testament.
54 Sirach 6:26-28, P. 776, The Old Testament.
55 Wisdom 8:9, P. 757, The Old Testament.
56 Wisdom 8:16, P. 757, The Old Testament.
57 Wisdom 8:2-3, P. 757, The Old Testament.
58 Sirach 4:11-18, P. 774-775, The Old Testament.
59 Baruch 4:1-2, P. 968, The Old Testament.
60 Job 28:20-23, P. 590, The Old Testament.
61 Wisdom 7:25-26, P. 756, The Old Testament.
62 Revelation 12:1-3, P. 398, The New Testament.
63 Exodus 15:20-21, P. 74, The Old Testament.
64 Luke 19:40, P. 133, The New Testament.
65 Song of Songs 1:5-6.
66 Wisdom 9:17-18.

AFTERWORD

67 Gloria L. Scwabb, SSJ, *"The Power of Presence: Toward a Shekhinah Christology"*, (Fordham University, December 2001).
68 Nehemiah 9: 12, p. 463, The Old Testament.
69 Wisdom 7:25-26, p. 756, The Old Testament.
70 Carolyn Woman Sur, *Feminine Images of God in the Visions of Hildegard of Bingen's Scivias*, (Lewiston: The Edwin Mellen Press, 1993) p. 10.
71 Joseph Campbell, *The Power of Myth*, (New York: Doubleday, 1988) p. 169.
72 Proverbs 8:27-31, p. 709, The Old Testament.

Books, Card Sets,
CDs & DVDs
that inspire and uplift

For a complete catalogue,
please contact:

Findhorn Press Ltd
305a The Park, Findhorn
Forres IV36 3TE
Scotland, UK

Telephone
+44-1309-690582
Fax
+44-1309-690036
eMail
info@findhornpress.com

or consult our catalogue online
(with secure order facility) on
www.findhornpress.com